ACE YOUR
FOOD
SCIENCE PROJECT

Titles in the

ACE YOUR SCIENCE PROJECT

series:

Ace Your Chemistry Science Project:
Great Science Fair Ideas

ISBN-13: 978-0-7660-3227-9
ISBN-10:   0-7660-3227-2

Ace Your Ecology and
Environmental Science Project:
Great Science Fair Ideas

ISBN-13: 978-0-7660-3216-3
ISBN-10:   0-7660-3216-7

Ace Your Food Science Project:
Great Science Fair Ideas

ISBN-13: 978-0-7660-3228-6
ISBN-10:   0-7660-3228-0

Ace Your Science Project Using
Chemistry Magic and Toys:
Great Science Fair Ideas

ISBN-13: 978-0-7660-3226-2
ISBN-10:   0-7660-3226-4

Ace Your Space Science Project:
Great Science Fair Ideas

ISBN-13: 978-0-7660-3230-9
ISBN-10:   0-7660-3230-2

A⁺ ACE YOUR SCIENCE PROJECT

ACE YOUR FOOD SCIENCE PROJECT

Robert Gardner,
Salvatore Tocci, and
Thomas R. Rybolt

GREAT SCIENCE FAIR IDEAS

Enslow Publishers, Inc.
40 Industrial Road
Box 398
Berkeley Heights, NJ 07922
USA

http://www.enslow.com

Library of Congress Cataloging-in-Publication Data

Gardner, Robert, 1929–
    Ace your food science project : great science fair ideas / Robert Gardner, Salvatore Tocci,
        and Thomas R. Rybolt.
        p. cm. — (Ace your science project)
    Includes bibliographical references and index.
        Summary: "Presents several science experiments and project ideas using food"—Provided
        by publisher.
    ISBN-13: 978-0-7660-3228-6
    ISBN-10: 0-7660-3228-0
    1. Food—Analysis—Juvenile literature. 2. Science projects—Juvenile literature.
        I. Tocci, Salvatore. II. Rybolt, Thomas R. III. Title.
    TX541.G37 2010
    664—dc22
                                                                    2008049780
Printed in the United States of America

10 9 8 7 6 5 4 3 2 1

To Our Readers: We have done our best to make sure all Internet addresses in this book were active and appropriate when we went to press. However, the author and the publisher have no control over and assume no liability for the material available on those Internet sites or on other Web sites they may link to. Any comments or suggestions can be sent by e-mail to comments@enslow.com or to the address on the back cover.

✪ Enslow Publishers, Inc., is committed to printing our books on recycled paper. The paper in every book contains 10% to 30% post-consumer waste (PCW). The cover board on the outside of each book contains 100% PCW. Our goal is to do our part to help young people and the environment too!

The experiments in this book are a collection of the authors' best experiments, which were previously published by Enslow Publishers, Inc., in *Health Science Projects About Nutrition, Science Fair Success Using Supermarket Products, Science Projects About Kitchen Chemistry*, and *Soda Pop Science Projects*.

Photo Credits: Shutterstock

Illustration Credits: All illustrations by Stephen F. Delisle, except Figure 23 by Tom LaBaff.

Cover Photos: All photos from Shutterstock, except trophy icons © bubaone/iStockphoto.com, and backgrounds © Chen Fu Soh/iStockphoto.com.

CONTENTS

Introduction 7
The Scientific Method 8
Science Fairs 10
Safety First 11

CHAPTER 1

Food, Energy, and Humans   13

🕐1.1 Drying Food 15
🕐1.2 Where Did That Food Come From? 18
🕐1.3 Where Do Carbohydrates Come From? 23
   1.4 Testing for Carbohydrates 27
   1.5 How Does Heat Affect Carbohydrates? 30
🕐1.6 The Energy Stored in a Corn Puff 36

CHAPTER 2

Fats, Proteins, Vitamins, and Minerals   41

🕐2.1 Testing for Fatty Food 43
   2.2 Testing for Proteins 47
   2.3 Proteins and the Tyndall Effect 49
🕐2.4 Testing for Vitamin C 57

CHAPTER 3

Yeast, Baking Soda, and Baking Powder   61

🕐3.1 Yeast: The Baker's and Brewer's Favorite Organisms 62
🕐3.2 Yeast and Different Sugars 67
🕐3.3 Yeast as a Catalyst 69
🕐3.4 Baking Soda 73
🕐3.5 The Many Uses of Baking Soda 76

CHAPTER 4

Dairy Products   81

🕐4.1 How Can You Turn Milk Into Cheese? 83
🕐4.2 Can You Measure How Unsaturated a Fat Is? ... 91
   4.3 What Is the Mineral Content of Milk? 97
   4.4 How Can You Mix Oil and Vinegar? 99

🕐 *Indicates experiments that offer ideas for science fair projects.*

CHAPTER 5

Fruits, Vegetables, Gelatin, Meat, and Carbonated Drinks

101

5.1 How Can You Keep Fruits and Salads Fresh? 103

◎5.2 How Can You Prevent Vegetables From Wilting? 105

5.3 How Do Enzymes Affect Gelatin? 108

5.4 How Does Meat Tenderizer Affect Protein? 110

◎5.5 Where's the Beef? 111

◎5.6 How Much Gas Is in a Bottle of Soda? 117

◎5.7 How Long Does a Fizzy Foam Last? 121

Further Reading and Internet Addresses 125

Index 126

◎ *Indicates experiments that offer ideas for science fair projects.*

INTRODUCTION

When you hear the word *science*, do you think of a person in a white lab coat surrounded by beakers of bubbling liquids, specialized lab equipment, and computers? What exactly is science? Maybe you think science is only a subject you learn in school. Science is much more than that.

Science is the study of the things that are all around you, every day. No matter where you are or what you are doing, scientific principles are at work. You don't need special materials or equipment, or even a white lab coat, to be a scientist. Materials commonly found in your home, at school, or at a local store will allow you to become a scientist and pursue an area of interest. By making careful observations and asking questions about how things work, you can begin to design experiments to investigate a variety of questions. You can do science. You probably already have but just didn't know it!

Perhaps you are reading this book because you are looking for an idea for a science fair project for school, or maybe you are just hoping to find something fun to do on a rainy day. This book will provide an opportunity for you to learn more about food and the field of food science. You may not realize that food is a science. You probably don't think too much about the food you eat. You probably don't often consider where it came from, how it was produced, what it is made of, or how much energy it contains. Food science is an important field that covers all aspects of harvesting, handling, processing, distributing, marketing, and consuming food. This field integrates and applies knowledge from chemistry, biology, microbiology, biochemistry, engineering, and nutrition for the production of safe, wholesome, and affordable food.

From the experiments in this book, you will discover the science behind many of the foods you eat every day. You may be surprised that you can have fun and learn about food science at the same time.

THE SCIENTIFIC METHOD

All scientists look at the world and try to understand how things work. They make careful observations and conduct research about a question. Different areas of science use different approaches. Depending on the phenomenon being investigated, one method is likely to be more appropriate than another. Designing a new medication for heart disease, studying the spread of an invasive plant species such as purple loosestrife, and finding evidence about whether there was once water on Mars all require different methods.

Despite the differences, however, all scientists use a similar general approach to do experiments. It is called the scientific method. In most experiments, some or all of the following steps are used: making an observation, formulating a question, making a hypothesis (an answer to the question) and prediction (an if-then statement), designing and conducting an experiment, analyzing results and drawing conclusions, and accepting or rejecting the hypothesis. Scientists then share their findings with others by writing articles that are published in journals. After—and only after—a hypothesis has repeatedly been supported by experiments can it be considered a theory.

You might be wondering how to get an experiment started. When you observe something in the world, you may become curious and think of a question. Your question can be answered by a well-designed investigation. Your question may also arise from an earlier experiment or from background reading. Once you have a question, you should make a hypothesis. Your hypothesis is a possible answer to the question (what you think will happen). Once you have a hypothesis, it is time to design an experiment.

In some cases, it is appropriate to do a controlled experiment. That means there are two groups treated exactly the same except for the single factor that you are testing. Any factor that can affect the outcome of an experiment is a *variable*. For example, if you want to investigate whether raisins will rise to the surface when placed in a carbonated beverage, two groups may be used. One group is called the control group, and the other is called the experimental group. The two groups should be treated exactly the same: The same number of raisins should be placed in the same amount of liquid, be kept at the same temperature, and so forth. The control group will be the raisins placed in sugar water, while the experimental group will be the raisins placed in ginger ale. The variable of interest is carbonation. It is the variable that changes, and it is the only difference between the two groups.

During the experiment, you will collect data. For example, you might count the number of raisins that rise to the surface. You might time how long it takes for the raisins to rise. By comparing the data collected from the control group with the data collected from the experimental group, you can draw conclusions. Because the two groups were treated exactly alike, all the raisins in the ginger ale rising to the surface would allow you to conclude with confidence that it is a result of the one thing that was different: carbonation.

Two other terms that are often used in scientific experiments are *dependent* and *independent* variables. The dependent variable here is the rising of raisins, because it is the one you measure as an outcome. Carbonation is the independent variable; it is the one the experimenter intentionally changes. After the data is collected, it is analyzed to see whether the hypothesis was supported or rejected. Often, the results of one experiment will lead you to a related question, or they may send you off in a different direction. Whatever the results, there is something to be learned from all scientific experiments.

SCIENCE FAIRS

Many of the experiments in this book may be appropriate for science fair projects. Experiments marked with a symbol (⚲) include a section called Science Fair Project Ideas. The ideas in this section will provide suggestions to help you develop your own original science fair project. However, judges at such fairs do not reward projects or experiments that are simply copied from a book. For example, a picture of the food pyramid, which is commonly found at these fairs, would probably not impress judges unless it was done in a novel or creative way. On the other hand, a carefully performed experiment to determine the amount of energy in a variety of snack foods would be likely to receive careful consideration.

Science fair judges tend to reward creative thought and imagination. However, it's difficult to be creative or imaginative unless you are really interested in your project. Take the time to choose a topic that appeals to you. Consider, too, your own ability and the cost of materials. Don't pursue a project that you can't afford.

If you decide to use a project found in this book for a science fair, you will need to find ways to modify or extend it. This should not be difficult because you will probably find that as you do these projects new ideas for experiments will come to mind. These new experiments could make excellent science fair projects, particularly because they spring from your own mind and are interesting to you.

If you decide to enter a science fair and have never done so before, you should read some of the books listed in the "Further Reading" section. The books that deal specifically with science fairs will provide plenty of helpful hints and lots of useful information that will enable you to avoid the pitfalls that sometimes plague first-time entrants. You will learn how to prepare appealing reports that include charts and graphs, how to set up and display your work, how to present your project, and how to relate to judges and visitors.

SAFETY FIRST

As with many activities, safety is important in science, and certain rules apply when conducting experiments. Some of the rules below may seem obvious to you, while others may not, but each is important to follow.

1. Have **an adult** help you whenever the book advises.

2. Wear eye protection and closed-toe shoes (rather than sandals) and tie back long hair.

3. Don't eat or drink while doing experiments and never taste substances being used unless instructed to do so.

4. Avoid touching chemicals.

5. Keep flammable substances away from fire.

6. When doing these experiments, use only nonmercury thermometers, such as those filled with alcohol. The liquid in some thermometers is mercury. It is dangerous to breathe mercury vapor. If you have mercury thermometers, **ask an adult** to take them to a local mercury thermometer exchange location.

7. Do only those experiments that are described in the book or those that have been approved by **an adult**.

8. Never engage in horseplay or play practical jokes.

9. Before beginning, read through the entire experimental procedure to make sure you understand all instructions. Clear extra items from your work space.

10. At the end of every activity, clean all materials used and put them away. Wash your hands thoroughly with soap and water.

Chapter 1

Food, Energy, and Humans

AFTER OUR HUMAN ANCESTORS BEGAN WALKING ON TWO LEGS, MOST OF THEIR WAKING HOURS WERE DEVOTED TO GATHERING FOOD. They ate fruits, nuts, roots, seeds, and mushrooms they gathered. Occasionally, they ate the meat of small animals they hunted or trapped. Sometimes they dined on the carcass of larger animals killed by a lion, leopard, or tiger, from which they would scavenge some meat and bones. The broken animal bones found at early human sites indicate that early humans especially sought the marrow found inside bones. Its fatty tissue served as a rich source of energy.

We do not know when humans first controlled fire, but it was probably more than a million years ago. Light from fires kept predators away and enabled the humans to work for longer periods. Fire also changed their diet. At some point, they probably ate the meat of a wild animal that had been burned in a forest fire and discovered that cooking improved the meat's flavor. Cooking also made food softer and easier to digest, and the poisons found in some plants and seeds could be broken down by high temperatures. Parasites and bacteria in meat were killed by the heat, so the meat could be preserved for short periods. Later, they discovered that meat could be preserved for a long time by smoking and drying it. Dried meat provided nourishment during winters in Europe, when deep snow prevented hunting or food gathering.

As their technology improved, the men became predominantly hunters. The women probably stayed at a home site, caring for the young and gathering fruits, nuts, tubers, and other foods from nearby. All the food was brought to a home base. There it was shared by all members of a social group that quite likely included the children and any elderly or ill people who were unable to hunt or gather. Gathering to eat at a home site is a unique human trait that persists to this day.

The large brains that made us human and social came with a price. Brain cells require extremely large amounts of energy. Brain tissue makes up only 2 percent of our weight, but it accounts for 20 percent of the energy we need. Food in the form of leaves, roots, fruit, and berries comes in small portions. It contains relatively small amounts of energy per volume eaten. Meat, on the other hand, is a rich source of energy. To meet the energy needs of their larger brains, early humans became more carnivorous. Fortunately, their larger brains provided the intelligence they needed to become better tool makers. With tools such as spears and knives, they were able to hunt animals they could not outrun or overpower. Tools allowed these early humans to increase the meat content of their diets and thereby provide the energy their larger brains required.

🏆 1.1 Drying Food

Materials:

- an adult
- ripe banana
- balance or kitchen scale
- knife
- lemon juice
- cookie sheet
- oven
- clock or watch
- spatula
- oven mitt
- plastic bags
- freezer
- refrigerator
- breadbox
- twist ties

Our ancestors dried food to preserve it for times when food was scarce. You can see how they did this by drying a banana. To begin, peel a ripe banana and cut off the ends of the fruit. Place the peeled banana on a plastic bag, weigh it, and record the weight. Then cut the banana into slices about 0.5 cm (1/4 in) thick. Dip each piece into some lemon juice. (You will learn the reason for the lemon juice when you do Experiment 5.1.) Place the slices in a single layer on a cookie sheet.

With an adult's supervision, preheat an oven to 60°C (140°F). Place the cookie sheet in the oven and leave it there for 30 minutes. Then open the oven and turn the banana slices over with a spatula. Continue to do this at 30-minute intervals until the slices no longer stick to the metal. After that, stir the slices at 30-minute intervals.

After 8 hours, remove the cookie sheet and let the banana slices cool. Once they are cool, place them on the plastic bag you used before and weigh them. What happened to the banana's weight? Can you explain why? By what percentage did the banana's weight change?

Taste one of the dried banana slices. Describe the flavor. Early humans probably used the sun to dry food and then kept it in a cool space underground, in a deep cave, or outside in the freezing cold of winter. Place a few of the banana slices in different plastic bags and seal with twist ties. Put the slices in different places such as a freezer, refrigerator, or breadbox. Which banana slices seem to remain unchanged for the longest time?

Science Fair Project Idea

Repeat this experiment with a number of different foods. Which of the foods you test have the largest percentage of water? Which foods contain very little water?

ENERGY FROM FOOD

To provide the energy needed to make a car go, you have to put gasoline into its tank. The gasoline is then burned in the cylinders of the engine to provide the energy needed to move the pistons up and down. The motion of the pistons is transferred to the wheels and the car moves. In a somewhat similar way, you eat food that passes to your stomach and intestines, where it is digested. The digested food is carried by blood to all the cells of your body. In the cells, the digested food is "burned" to provide energy. This energy is needed so that your body can move and carry on all the chemical activities that go on inside you.

Unlike the fuel you put into a car, not all the food you eat is "burned" to produce energy. Some of it is used to build new cells—new bone, new muscle, new skin, new blood cells, new fat cells. Some kinds of food provide only energy, while others allow you to grow or replace cells that die or wear out. There are also substances (chemicals) that regulate and maintain all the many processes that go on in your body. So what you eat is as important—or more important—than how much you eat.

Food is any substance we eat that provides us with energy, the materials we need to grow new tissue or replace old tissue, or to regulate the chemical reactions and physical processes that take place in our bodies.

We obtain food from the cells that make up plant and animal tissues or from substances that these organisms produce. For example, we may eat beef, which is the muscle tissue of cows. Or we may drink milk, which is a substance secreted by cows. We can eat the flowers of zucchini plants (their petals are delicious when fried in butter and flour), or we can wait and eat the fruit (zucchini squash) that result when the eggs in the flowers are fertilized.

Some people are vegetarians. They obtain all their food from plants or plant products. Some vegetarians eat animal products, such as milk, butter, yogurt, and honey, but not meat. Other vegetarians eat only plants or plant products.

While you do the experiment that follows, think about the source of the food that you eat.

Materials:
-friends from
different cultures

On a particular day, make a vertical list of everything that you eat and drink for breakfast, lunch, dinner, and between meals. Beside each of the items you ate, record the source of that food. Was it from a plant? (Do not forget that plants produce the grains found in bread, cakes, crackers, and other foods made with flour.) Was it something produced by an animal? If so, what was the animal that produced it?

Did you eat any nonfood substances, such as artificial coloring? If so, what were those substances? If they are not food, why did you eat them?

Keep a record of all the different kinds of food you eat during a one-week period. Ask a friend from a different culture to keep a similar record. Then compare the foods in the two lists. Are there foods in your friend's list that you do not recognize? Are there foods in your list that your friend does not recognize?

With your parents' permission, invite your friend to dinner and prepare one of the foods unfamiliar to your friend. Does he or she like the food? If you are lucky, your friend will invite you to dinner so that you can experience the taste of a food you have never eaten before.

You might also enjoy eating at restaurants that specialize in Indian, African, Thai, Chinese, Mexican, Italian, or other foreign foods. Which foods do you like? Which would you not order again?

Science Fair Project Ideas

- Interview a number of vegetarians. Why do they not eat meat? Why do some eat animal products, such as cheese, while others do not?
- Research how far your food traveled to reach you. How much of your food comes from your own state? How much energy was used to process and ship your food? Are there advantages to eating food that was produced locally?

FOODS

Energy is stored in the molecules of the food we eat. In our cells, the molecules react with oxygen, which is carried from our lungs to all the cells of our body by our blood. The reaction between these food molecules and oxygen is not a simple one, such as that in burning wood. It is, in fact, a series of reactions, each of which provides some energy.

There are three types of food that can provide the body with energy. They are *carbohydrates, fats,* and *proteins*. Carbohydrates and fats provide most of the energy, but only proteins contain the chemicals our bodies need to make new cells and repair old ones. The processes by which we use food to obtain energy, grow new tissue, and repair old tissue depend on certain other essential nutrients known as vitamins and minerals.

Of course, we also need water, which makes up well over half the weight of our bodies. More than two-thirds of the food we eat is actually water. The water we ingest comes from three sources: the liquids we drink, foods that contain water, and water produced in the body by chemical reactions that take place there. For example, when we "burn" sugar to obtain energy, water is produced as a by-product.

CARBOHYDRATES: A SOURCE OF ENERGY

Carbohydrates are the most abundant and economical of the three foods. Carbohydrates are compounds; that is, they are made of elements that have combined chemically in a particular ratio. The *carbo-* part of the term *carbohydrate* tells you that these compounds contain carbon. The *-hydrate* part indicates the presence of water. Since water contains hydrogen and oxygen, carbohydrates consist of the elements carbon (C), hydrogen (H), and oxygen (O). (The letters in parentheses are the chemical symbols for the elements named.) In carbohydrates, there are two hydrogen atoms for every oxygen atom, just as there are in water (H_2O).

Carbohydrates are either simple sugars, such as glucose, dextrose, fructose, or levulose, or substances that will react with water to form simple sugars. The simple sugars are called monosaccharides (see Figure 1a).

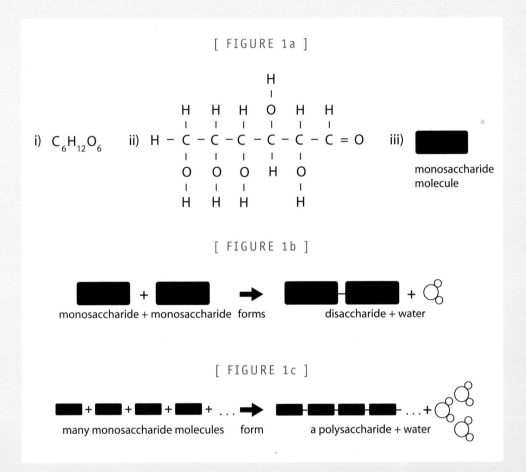

[FIGURE 1a]

i) $C_6H_{12}O_6$

ii)
$$H - \overset{\overset{\displaystyle H}{|}}{C} - \overset{\overset{\displaystyle H}{|}}{\underset{\underset{\displaystyle H}{|}}{\underset{\displaystyle O}{}}} - \overset{\overset{\displaystyle H}{|}}{\underset{\underset{\displaystyle H}{|}}{\underset{\displaystyle O}{}}} - \overset{\overset{\displaystyle O}{|}}{\underset{\underset{\displaystyle H}{|}}{\underset{\displaystyle O}{}}} - \overset{\overset{\displaystyle H}{|}}{\underset{\underset{\displaystyle H}{|}}{\underset{\displaystyle H}{}}} - \overset{\overset{\displaystyle H}{|}}{\underset{\underset{\displaystyle H}{|}}{\underset{\displaystyle O}{}}} = O$$

iii) monosaccharide molecule

[FIGURE 1b]

monosaccharide + monosaccharide forms   disaccharide + water

[FIGURE 1c]

many monosaccharide molecules   form   a polysaccharide + water

1 a) A molecule of a monosaccharide, or simple sugar, such as glucose contains 6 carbon atoms, 12 hydrogen atoms, and 6 oxygen atoms. The molecule can be represented in several different ways: i) The molecular formula for a monosaccharide; ii) A structural formula showing how the atoms in glucose, a particular sugar, are arranged; iii) A rectangle can be used to represent any monosaccharide molecule. b) Two monosaccharide molecules combine to form a disaccharide molecule and a molecule of water. c) Many monosaccharide molecules combine to form a polysaccharide molecule, such as starch, while producing a molecule of water each time a monosaccharide is added.

The monosaccharides found in foods such as fruits have 6 carbon atoms, 12 hydrogen atoms, and 6 oxygen atoms ($C_6H_{12}O_6$). All these simple sugars have these same numbers of atoms of carbon, hydrogen, and oxygen. The compounds are different, however, because their atoms are arranged differently. Their arrangement is shown in their structural formula (see Figure 1aii).

Disaccharide molecules (Figure 1b) form when two monosaccharide molecules combine and lose a molecule of water. The molecules of sucrose—ordinary table sugar—form a disaccharide. Sucrose has 12 carbon atoms, 22 hydrogen atoms, and 11 oxygen atoms ($C_{12}H_{22}O_{11}$). Lactose, the sugar found in milk, and maltose, the sugar found in malts and germinating cereals, are also disaccharides. Disaccharides must be changed (digested) to monosaccharides in your body before their energy can be tapped.

Polysaccharides (Figure 1c) are molecules made of many units of monosaccharide sugars joined together. Each monosaccharide molecule loses a molecule of water when it joins the polysaccharide chain. The most common polysaccharide in food is starch, which is stored in plant cells, and cellulose, which makes up the cell walls in plants. When our bodies digest starch, the starch is changed to simple sugars; that is, the polysaccharide molecules are converted to monosaccharide molecules. Humans are unable to digest cellulose. However, cellulose provides fiber, which helps to move food through the intestines. Unlike plants, we store carbohydrates as glycogen, another polysaccharide that is found in our livers and muscles.

Materials:

- an adult
- paper clip
- black construction paper or aluminum foil
- geranium plant
- gloves or oven mitt
- safety glasses
- tongs
- stove
- pan
- water
- rubbing alcohol
- small jar
- tincture of iodine
- measuring teaspoon

Our bodies are not able to make sugars and starches (carbohydrates). Only plants with the green pigment chlorophyll can manufacture carbohydrates. Most of the carbohydrates we eat come from plants. If you look at the list of the food you ate from Experiment 1.2, you will find that the foods came either (1) from plants or (2) from animals that ate plants or plant products such as grain.

The leaves of plants are food factories. Cells in the leaves take carbon dioxide gas from the air and combine it with water in the presence of light to make sugar, which is stored in plant cells as starch. The carbon dioxide provides the carbon and oxygen found in carbohydrates, and the water provides the hydrogen. During this process, which is called photo-synthesis, plants release oxygen into the atmosphere. The oxygen also comes from the water.

Leaves are green because they contain pigments that absorb most of the colors in white light except green. Because green light is reflected instead of being absorbed, most leaves appear green. A pigment is a colored substance. The green pigment in plant cells that is essential to photosynthesis is chlorophyll. Chlorophyll absorbs light, which is converted to the energy stored in molecules of starch during photosynthesis.

Any excess sugar produced in a leaf is changed to starch and stored. You can use a common test for starch to confirm that food is produced in leaves when light, carbon dioxide, and water are present. Use a paper clip to hold a small folded piece of black construction paper or aluminum foil over both sides of a geranium leaf still on the plant, as shown in Figure 2. Be careful not to damage the leaf when you attach the paper or foil. Do this in the morning on a bright sunny day when lots of light will fall on the leaves.

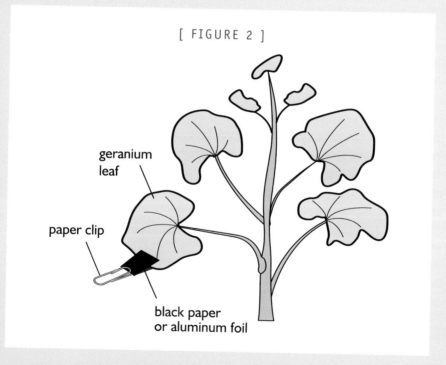

[FIGURE 2]

geranium leaf

paper clip

black paper or aluminum foil

Use black paper or aluminum foil to prevent light from reaching part of a geranium leaf.

After four or five hours, pick the leaf from the plant, bring it indoors, and remove the foil or paper. Put on gloves or an oven mitt and safety glasses. Then, **under adult supervision,** use tongs to hold the leaf's stem so that you can immerse the rest of the leaf into a pan of boiling water on a stove. Hold the leaf under the boiling water for about a minute. The heat will break open cell walls within the leaf.

Now that the cell walls are broken, you can remove the green chlorophyll from the leaf. But first turn off the stove. **Caution: The rubbing alcohol you will use to extract the pigments is flammable. It should never be brought near a flame or red-hot burner.**

Prepare a small jar of rubbing alcohol, place the limp leaf in it, and leave it overnight. The next morning you will find the alcohol has a green color due to the pigments it has extracted from the leaf.

In a saucer, mix together equal amounts of tincture of iodine and water; about 5 milliliters (ml) (1 teaspoon) of each will do. **Remember: Iodine is poisonous. Handle it carefully!** Next, rinse the leaf in warm water to remove the alcohol. Then spread it out and place it in the iodine-water solution.

If the leaf contained starch, you will see it turn a dark blue-black color—the color that forms when iodine reacts with starch. Was there starch in the leaf cells? Is one area of the leaf much lighter than the rest? Can you identify that region? In which area of the leaf did photosynthesis not take place? What evidence do you have to show that light is required for photosynthesis?

Science Fair Project Ideas

How do we know that the oxygen released during photosynthesis comes from the water in the plant and not from the carbon dioxide, or not from both water and carbon dioxide?

- Design an experiment to show that plants need carbon dioxide in order to perform photosynthesis. Then, **under adult supervision**, carry out your experiment.
- Design an experiment to show that chlorophyll is needed for plants to perform photosynthesis. Then, **under adult supervision**, carry out your experiment.

Materials:

-an adult

-saucers

-eyedropper

-tincture of iodine

-water

-cornstarch

-potato

-bread

-milk

-cooked white meat

-unsalted crackers

-Clinistix (from a drug store); or Benedict's solution (from school)

-stove

-small cooking pan

-measuring teaspoons (1 and ¼)

-corn syrup or maple syrup

-test tube or small glass

-sucrose (table sugar)

-toothpicks

TESTING FOR STARCH

From the previous experiment, you know that iodine can be used to test for starch. Prepare a dilute iodine solution by mixing about 10 drops of tincture of iodine with 100 drops of water. **Be careful handling iodine. It is a poison.**

You can use this iodine solution to test for starch in foods. In separate saucers, crush or pour samples of potato, bread, milk, cooked white meat such as chicken breast, and a piece of an unsalted cracker. Into still another container, spit out a piece of another unsalted cracker that you have chewed for about five minutes.

Mix each of the food samples with a little water. Then test each sample with a drop of the iodine solution. **Remember not to put anything with iodine on it into your mouth!**

Which foods contain starch? What other foods might you try?

TESTING FOR SUGAR

If you can obtain Clinistix from a drug store, you can use them to test for simple sugars. Just dip the stick in a sample of liquid that you think may contain simple sugars. If Clinistix are not available, your school may have Benedict's solution. **With your teacher's permission**, you can use Benedict's solution to test for simple sugars. Pour about 5 ml (1 tsp) of corn syrup or maple syrup into a test tube or a small glass. Add about 5 ml (1 tsp) of the Benedict's solution and place the tube or glass in a small pan that holds some water. **With an adult's help**, place the pan on a stove and heat the water to boiling. If a simple (monosaccharide) sugar is present, the liquid will turn green, yellow, red, or orange. An orange color indicates a high concentration of simple sugar.

Repeat the experiment using 5 ml (1 tsp) of a saturated solution of sucrose (table sugar). Does this sugar solution contain any simple sugars?

In separate dishes, crush samples of potato, bread, milk, and cooked white meat. Into another dish spit out an unsalted cracker that you have chewed for about five minutes. Mix each of these samples with a little water and test with Clinistix or Benedict's solution as you did previously.

Mix 1/4 teaspoon of cornstarch with an equal amount of corn syrup or maple syrup, each of which, as you know from an earlier test, contains a simple sugar. Add some water and stir the mixture with a toothpick. Pour a small amount of the mixture onto a saucer and add a drop of iodine solution. **Remember: Iodine is poisonous!** Do you get a positive test for starch when it is mixed with sugar? Test for a simple sugar with Clinistix or, **under your teacher's supervision**, test using Benedict's solution. Do you get a positive test for a simple sugar when it is mixed with starch?

Materials:
- an adult
- heavy-duty aluminum foil
- clothespin
- table sugar (sucrose)
- candle and candle holder
- safety glasses
- oven mitt
- matches
- a friend
- metal cooking pan
- water
- cobalt chloride paper strips (you may be able to borrow from your school)
- cornstarch
- flour
- bread
- raw potato
- corn syrup
- unflavored gelatin powder
- measuring cup
- measuring teaspoon
- watercolor brush
- sugar
- white paper
- tongs

Carbohydrates?

Many compounds can be broken down (decomposed) into simpler substances by heating them. From what you know about their composition, what do you predict will happen if you decompose a carbohydrate by heating it?

To test your prediction, make a number of small pans with handles by folding pieces of heavy-duty aluminum foil, as shown in Figure 3a. Use a clothespin to grasp the pan's handle. This will allow you to safely hold the pan over a flame. Place a very small amount of ordinary sugar (sucrose) in one of the pans. Place a candle in a candle holder. **Put safety glasses over your eyes and an oven mitt on your hand.** Then, **under adult supervision**, light the candle and heat the sugar by holding the pan above the candle flame, as shown in Figure 3b.

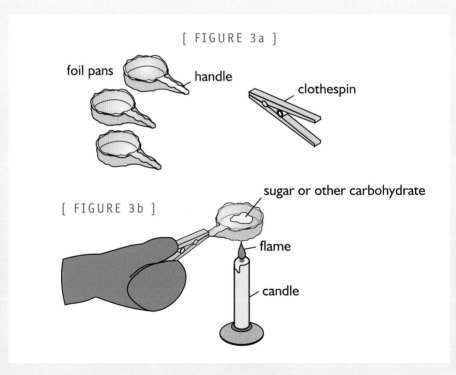

[FIGURE 3a]

foil pans   handle   clothespin

sugar or other carbohydrate

[FIGURE 3b]

flame

candle

3 a) **Make small pans by folding pieces of heavy-duty aluminum foil.**
   b) **Use a clothespin to hold a pan with a sample of sugar over a flame.**

What happens to the sugar when you heat it? Is there any evidence of vapor coming from the decomposing sugar? If there is, ask a friend to hold a cooking pan of cold water over the vapor. Does any liquid condense on the bottom of the pan? If it does, what do you think that liquid might be?

If strips of blue cobalt chloride paper are available, place the end of a strip in the liquid. Cobalt chloride paper turns pink in water. Can you identify the liquid now? What confirming tests might you do?

Did the sugar change? Does it eventually turn black? What do you think the black substance is?

Repeat the experiment, this time with a very small amount of cornstarch in place of the sugar. What happens to the cornstarch when you heat it?

Try heating very small amounts of other carbohydrates and carbohydrate-rich foods such as flour, bread, raw potato, and a drop of corn syrup. What seems to be the common substance that remains after all these carbohydrates are heated? What else do you think is produced when these carbohydrates decompose?

Do other foods behave in the same way? To find out, you might try heating a protein such as gelatin powder. Does the gelatin powder decompose in a way similar to carbohydrate decomposition?

Heating a food to decompose it is the secret of many invisible inks. Dissolve a teaspoonful of sugar in 60 ml (2 oz) of hot water. Using a watercolor paintbrush as a pen and the sugar solution as ink, write a short message on a piece of white paper. After the "ink" has dried, heat the paper **under adult supervision** by holding it with tongs above a candle flame. Why does the message slowly appear?

MEASURING ENERGY: THE CALORIE

There are many forms of energy—light, gravitational, kinetic, electrical, elastic, and so on. All these different forms of energy can be converted to heat (thermal energy). Consequently, heat is a useful way to measure energy. You can measure heat in units known as calories. A calorie is the quantity of heat required to raise the temperature of 1 gram (g) of water by 1 degree Celsius (°C). If you add heat to water, the water's temperature will rise. If you remove heat from water, its temperature will fall. If the temperature of 1 g of water rises 1°C, 1 calorie of heat has been added to the water. If the temperature of 10 g of water rises 10°C, 100 calories of heat have been added. The product of the mass of the water and its temperature change can be used to measure heat.

Heat (in calories) = mass of water (in grams) × temperature change (in °C).

Nutritionists, dietitians, doctors, and other people who work with food need to know how much energy is stored in the foods people eat. They measure energy in Calories. Notice that the unit of energy they use is spelled with a capital C. It is sometimes called a large calorie, or a kilocalorie. It is equal to 1,000 calories. It is the heat required to raise the temperature of 1.0 kilogram (1,000 g) of water through 1°C. A dietitian may say that a tablespoon of peanut butter contains 90 Calories. He or she means that if the energy stored in that peanut butter were converted to heat, the heat generated would be enough to raise the temperature of 10 kg of water 9°C.

We say food is "burned" in our bodies; however, there are no flames. The food does combine with oxygen to produce carbon dioxide and water eventually. But it does so in a series of reactions. Each reaction releases a small amount of energy that keeps our bodies warm or allows our muscles to contract, our brains to think, and our cells to carry on the many processes that take place there. In the end, the total energy the food provides is equal to the heat it releases when it burns outside the body.

To find the energy available in a food, the food is weighed and placed in a metal container known as a bomb calorimeter (Figure 4). Oxygen is added to the calorimeter, which is surrounded by water. The outer wall of the calorimeter is well insulated so that very little heat can escape. The food is ignited, and it burns in the calorimeter. The heat released is

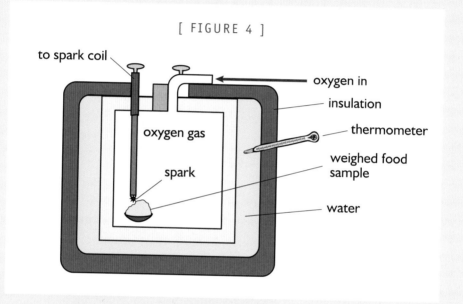

[FIGURE 4]

to spark coil

oxygen in

insulation

oxygen gas

thermometer

weighed food sample

spark

water

In a bomb calorimeter, a weighed sample of food is ignited by a spark. The food burns in oxygen and the heat released warms a known amount of water that surrounds the chamber where the food burns. By knowing the temperature change of the water, the heat released by the food can be calculated.

absorbed by the water surrounding the reaction. The change in the water's temperature when multiplied by the mass of the water allows the experimenter to determine the energy released when the food burns.

Suppose that 1.5 g of food burns. Its heat is absorbed by 1.0 kg of water, which undergoes a temperature change of 6.15°C. The heat released by the food is

$$1.0 \text{ kg} \times 6.15°C = 6.15 \text{ Cal.}$$

The heat released in terms of Calories per gram of food is

$$6.15 \text{ Cal} \div 1.5 \text{ g} = 4.1 \text{ Cal/g.}$$

The experimenter knows that the food that burned is a carbohydrate because carbohydrates typically release 4.1 Cal/g. A fat would have released 9.45 Cal/g, and a protein would have released 5.65 Cal/g. Protein, however, is never completely "burned" in the body. Some always remains in the form of urea, uric acid, or creatinine. These waste products, which still contain about 1.3 Cal/g, are excreted in the urine. As a result, our bodies can only obtain about 4.3 Cal/g from protein. Generally, nutritionists round off energy values and say that carbohydrates and proteins release about 4 Cal/g and fats provide 9 Cal/g.

SNACK FOODS

Your favorite aisles at a supermarket may be the ones with the snack foods, desserts, and candies. In fact, those aisles are probably the favorite ones for many people. Most everyone can recall a day when they devoured a large container of popcorn at the movies, downed a whole bag of pretzels at a picnic, or ate a bowl of potato chips while watching television. Although snack foods may satisfy our hunger, they provide only limited quantities of a few important nutrients. Moreover, if a person maintained a steady diet of those foods, the extra pounds would quickly begin to show. The same is true not only of snack foods but also of desserts and candies. The increased weight would result from the large number of calories present in these foods. In the next experiment, you will make your own calorimeter to measure the calories in breakfast cereals, nuts, and other snacks.

Materials:

- an adult
- small (180-ml or 6-oz) frozen juice can with a metal bottom and cardboard sides
- large nail
- pencil
- large (#10) tin can
- can opener
- cork
- aluminum foil
- pliers
- large sewing needle
- balance or scale
- cold water
- graduated cylinder or measuring cup
- laboratory thermometer (-10–110°C)
- matches
- corn puffs
- peanuts
- walnuts
- cashews

In your body, food is digested, absorbed into your blood, and carried to cells where it is oxidized slowly in a series of chemical reactions that release the energy stored in the molecules of food. You can find the energy stored in a piece of food by burning it in air or oxygen and measuring the energy released.

To find the energy stored in a corn puff, you can build a simple calorimeter like the one shown in Figure 5. A small, empty 180-ml (6-oz) frozen juice can with a metal bottom and cardboard sides can be used to hold

Corn Puff

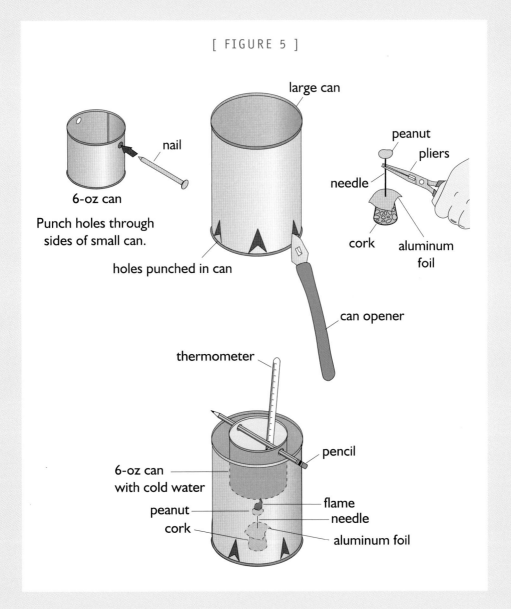

[FIGURE 5]

large can

nail

6-oz can

Punch holes through
sides of small can.

holes punched in can

peanut

pliers

needle

cork   aluminum
foil

can opener

thermometer

pencil

6-oz can
with cold water

peanut   flame
                          needle
cork
                          aluminum foil

The energy stored in food can be measured by burning the food and
capturing the heat released in a known amount of water.

cold water. **Ask an adult** to use a nail to punch holes through opposite sides of the can near its open top. Push a pencil through the holes. The pencil will support this small can inside a large (#10) can.

Ask an adult to remove both ends of the large can. Use a can opener to make four or five triangular holes along the sides of the large can near its bottom end, as shown in Figure 5. The holes will allow air to enter the can so the corn puff will burn. The bright interior of the large can will reflect heat that might otherwise escape to the surrounding air.

To support the corn puff, cover the small end of a cork with a piece of aluminum foil. With pliers, force the eye of a large sewing needle through the foil and into the cork, as shown. Next, break the corn puff in half. Weigh one of the halves on a sensitive balance. If the balance is not sensitive enough to weigh one corn puff, weigh a hundred of them and divide by 200 to find the weight of half of one. Next, push the corn puff half down gently onto the sharp, upright end of the needle. Pour 150 g (5 oz) of cold water into the small can. (Since 1.0 ml of water weighs 1 g, you now have 150 g of water in the can.) Place a laboratory (alcohol) thermometer in the can and measure the water's temperature.

Ask an adult to light the corn puff with a match. Immediately place the large can over the burning corn puff and put the small can with the water into the large can, as shown in Figure 5. Stir the water gently with the thermometer until after the corn puff goes out. Does any of the corn puff remain? If it does, can you identify what the remaining mass is?

Record the final temperature of the water. The mass of water and its temperature change can be used to calculate the heat released by the burning corn puff. Remember, a calorie is the amount of heat required to raise the temperature of 1 g of water by 1°C. If the temperature of the 150 g of water increased by 10°C, then the corn puff provided 1,500 calories (150 g x 10°C) of energy. How much heat did the burning corn puff release?

If any of the corn puff remains, reweigh it. What mass of corn puff, in grams, provided the heat absorbed by the water? How much heat was produced per gram of corn puff burned? Do you think the value of the heat per gram that you obtained from your data is higher or lower than the actual value? What makes you think so?

Nutritionists measure energy in Calories. A Calorie with a capital "C" is the heat needed to raise the temperature of 1 *kilogram* of water by 1°C, so it is 1,000 times bigger than a calorie with a small c. How many Calories are provided by 1 gram of corn puff according to your data?

Under adult supervision, find the heat released per gram, in calories per gram, by a peanut. Try a walnut, then a cashew. How do they each compare with the energy per gram of a corn puff?

Science Fair Project Idea

With an adult present, use the equipment you used in Experiment 1.6 to measure the amount of heat, in calories, released per gram of candle wax for several different kinds of candles. If we can obtain energy from candle wax, why don't we use it as a food?

Carbohydrates are found in bread and vegetables. Protein can be found in eggs and meats. Olive oil is an example of a fat. Your body needs all of these things to function properly.

Chapter 2

Fats, Proteins, Vitamins, and Minerals

CARBOHYDRATES MAKE UP THE BULK OF THE FOOD WE CONSUME AND PROVIDE MOST OF THE ENERGY OUR BODIES NEED. However, we cannot live for long on a diet of carbohydrates alone. We need protein to provide the matter needed for the growth and repair of cells. Enzymes that help digest food and regulate other chemical processes that take place within our bodies are also proteins. And we need at least small amounts of fat to make adipose tissue, the soft tissue that insulates our bodies and cushions our internal organs. Fat is also required to carry certain fat-soluble vitamins to our cells. Both fat-soluble and water-soluble vitamins are needed to regulate the many chemical reactions that go on within our bodies and make life possible. We also require a great variety of minerals, including calcium, iron, magnesium, and potassium. Macrominerals such as calcium, phosphorus, salt (sodium chloride), potassium, and magnesium are needed in relatively large amounts. For example, we require more than a gram of calcium and phosphorus each day to build and maintain our bones and teeth. Trace minerals, such as iron, iodine, and zinc, are essential to life, but only a few milligrams or less of them are needed in our daily diet. About 10 to 20 mg of iron is sufficient to combine with proteins to make the hemoglobin found in the red blood cells we produce continually in our bone marrow. And less than a milligram of iodine, readily provided by iodized salt, is needed to keep our thyroid glands functioning properly.

In this chapter, you will learn more about these various food substances. You will carry out experiments to test for the presence of fats and proteins, and you will use a chemical test to find out which juices have the largest concentration of vitamin C.

FATS: ANOTHER SOURCE OF ENERGY AND A MEANS OF STORING IT

Fats are compounds that contain carbon, hydrogen, and oxygen, but not in the same ratio as carbohydrates. If you have ever eaten overcooked bacon, you are aware that fat contains carbon, which is the black substance that remains after fat has been decomposed by heating. Fats contain more carbon and hydrogen but less oxygen per gram than carbohydrates. As a result, they provide more energy than carbohydrates or proteins.

If you eat more food than your body needs, the excess is stored as fat in cells that make up what is called adipose tissue. Everyone has some adipose tissue beneath the skin, as well as on and in internal organs such as the kidneys and intestines. The fat protects and cushions the organs and stores energy.

Materials:
- brown paper bag
- cooking oil
- water
- bacon
- hot dog
- peanut butter
- butter
- margarine
- lard
- milk
- walnut
- cream
- orange juice
- lemonade
- mayonnaise
- lowfat mayonnaise
- egg whites
- egg yolks

Chemists have ways of testing for fats, but their methods involve substances that are explosive or toxic. There is, however, one simple test that can be used to identify many fatty foods. Tear off one side of a brown paper bag. Put a drop of cooking oil on your finger and rub it in a circular fashion on one small section of the brown paper. Use another finger to rub some water into another part of the paper in the same way. If you hold the paper up to the light, you will see that the spot made with the cooking oil and, perhaps, the one made with water as well, are translucent—they transmit light. The liquids transmit light because they fill in the spaces between the wood fibers in the paper that trap the light. The water spot will become opaque as the liquid evaporates, but the oily spot, which contains fat, will remain translucent. What might explain why the oily spot remains translucent?

Try testing some other substances. Make circles on the brown paper using uncooked bacon and a slice of an uncooked hot dog. Try some peanut butter, ordinary butter, margarine, and lard. Also try milk, a walnut, cream, orange juice, lemonade, mayonnaise, lowfat mayonnaise, egg whites, and egg yolks. Which of these substances give a positive test for fat? Which appear to have little or no fat?

Always wash your hands with soap and warm water after handling uncooked meat or raw eggs.

Science Fair Project Idea

A photometer is a device that can be used to compare the brightness of two light sources, such as two light bulbs. Hold a piece of brown paper with a grease spot on it up to a light. What happens to the grease spot when the light on the far side is brighter than the near side? What happens when the light on the near side is brighter? Can you see the grease spot when the two light sources are balanced? Use the Internet to research the inverse square law. How does it apply to the observations made with your homemade photometer?

PROTEINS: FOOD FOR ENERGY AND FOR MAKING NEW TISSUE

In addition to carbon, hydrogen, and oxygen, proteins always contain nitrogen and sometimes sulfur, phosphorus, or iron. Protein molecules consist of chains of amino acid molecules joined together, as shown in Figure 6. These molecules are very large. A molecule of albumin, the protein found in egg white, weighs about as much as 2,400 water molecules. Hemoglobin molecules, one of the proteins found in red blood cells, weigh about 3,500 times as much as water molecules.

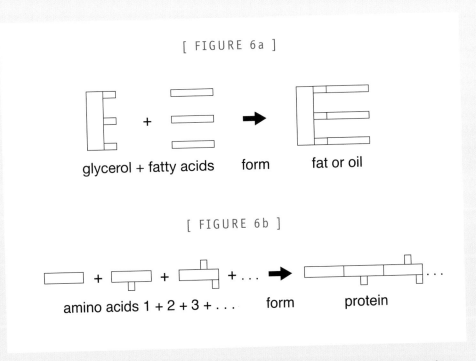

[FIGURE 6a]

glycerol + fatty acids   form   fat or oil

[FIGURE 6b]

amino acids 1 + 2 + 3 + . . .   form   protein

6 a) The structural and molecular formulas of glycine, one of the simplest amino acids, are shown. We can also represent an amino acid with a rectangle. b) Many amino acid molecules join together to form a protein molecule.

The proteins found in the human body are formed from 20 different amino acids. About half of those amino acids must be obtained from the food we eat. The others can be made from other substances in our diet. Rich sources of protein are milk, meat, fish, eggs, cereal, and some vegetables such as legumes (peas, beans, lentils, and peanuts).

Protein-rich foods are difficult and expensive to produce. That is one cause of malnutrition among people in poor countries. They cannot afford the protein they need to build, replace, or repair bone, muscle, and connective tissue.

Materials:

- science teacher
- safety glasses
- balance
- rubber gloves
- sodium hydroxide (NaOH) crystals (Obtain from school science laboratory.)
- copper sulfate crystals ($CuSO_4 \cdot 5H_2O$) (Obtain from school science laboratory.)
- cold water
- egg
- butter knife
- bowl
- soap
- 2 glass jars
- metric measuring cup or graduated cylinder
- large test tube or small jar or bottle
- stopper
- eyedropper
- flour
- gelatin
- potato
- bread
- milk
- cooked white meat of chicken
- crackers
- sugar

The Biuret test can be used to identify protein in food. Because the test involves the use of sodium hydroxide (lye) solution, which is harmful to skin and eyes, ask your science teacher to help you with this experiment. **Both you and your teacher should wear safety glasses and rubber gloves throughout the experiment.** Your teacher should prepare the sodium hydroxide (NaOH) solution by adding 10 g of the white solid to 100 ml of cold water and stirring until the solid is dissolved.

While the teacher is preparing the sodium hydroxide solution, you can prepare a 3-percent solution of copper sulfate by adding 3 g of blue copper sulfate ($CuSO_4 \bullet 5H_2O$) crystals to 100 ml of water.

Egg white from a raw egg is a good source of protein. It can be used to reveal what a positive test for protein looks like. Separate the white of an egg from its yolk. To do this, use a butter knife to crack an egg at its center. Hold the egg upright over a bowl. Remove the upper half of the shell. Some egg white will fall into the bowl when you remove the upper half of the shell. Now carefully pour the yolk, trying not to break it, from one half of the shell to the other several times over the bowl. As you do so, more egg white will fall into the bowl. When most of the white has been removed, discard the yolk, which is primarily fat, or save it for cooking. **Wash your hands after handling raw eggs.**

Pour the egg white into a large test tube or a small jar or bottle with a lid. Add an equal volume of water, stopper the tube, and shake it to mix the egg white and water thoroughly. **Have your teacher** add an equal volume of the sodium hydroxide solution; stopper and shake the tube again. Then add about 5 drops of the copper sulfate solution; stopper and shake once more. A violet or blue-violet color indicates the presence of protein. The darker the color, the greater the concentration of protein.

Mash samples of different foods separately in water. You might use flour, gelatin, pieces of potato, bread, milk, cooked white meat, crackers, and sugar. **Ask your teacher** to help you test these foods for protein. Which foods give a positive test for protein? Which foods can you conclude do not contain protein?

2.3 Proteins and the Tyndall Effect

Materials:
- measuring teaspoon
- sugar
- small glass or beaker
- warm water
- bowl
- knife
- spoon
- egg
- eyedropper
- small test tube
- glass of water
- dark area
- penlight or small flashlight
- water from streams, lakes, or rivers

John Tyndall was a nineteenth-century British physicist who discovered that if a beam of light passes through water or any clear liquid containing small molecules, the beam cannot be seen from the side of the clear vessel holding the liquid (see Figure 7a). Larger particles, however, do reflect some of the light, making the beam visible—just as a beam of sunlight can be seen when it shines through dust particles in a room.

To observe what Tyndall saw, pour a teaspoonful of sugar into a small glass or beaker. Fill the vessel about halfway with warm water and stir the mixture with a spoon. As you can see, the sugar dissolves in the water to form a clear solution.

Next, separate the white of an egg from the yolk, as described in Experiment 2.2. Use an eyedropper to transfer the egg white to a small test tube.

Take both liquids and a glass of water to a dark area. Use a penlight or a small flashlight to shine a narrow beam of light through the sugar solution while you view the liquid from the side, as shown in Figure 7.

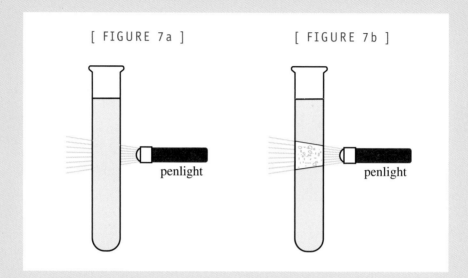

[FIGURE 7a]   [FIGURE 7b]

penlight   penlight

7 a) A beam of light passing through water or a clear solution cannot be seen from the side. The particles in the liquid are too small to reflect any light. b) Large particles do reflect some light, making the beam visible from the side.

If you can see the beam in the liquid when you view it from the side, you are observing what is known as the Tyndall effect (see Figure 7b).

Is there a Tyndall effect when you shine the light through the sugar solution? Is there a Tyndall effect when you shine the light through a glass of water?

Remembering that protein molecules, such as those found in egg white, are some of the largest molecules known, would you expect to observe the Tyndall effect when you shine the light through the egg white? Try it. Was your prediction correct?

Use the Tyndall effect to compare the amounts of mud in water from streams, lakes, or rivers near your home. Demonstrate differences in your project display.

MINERALS

There are 92 natural elements, but 96 percent of your body is composed of only four elements—oxygen, carbon, hydrogen, and nitrogen. The remaining 4 percent contains trace amounts of 60 different elements. The functions of some of these elements in the body are known. Other elements are probably essential for health, but their uses remain unknown.

The elements that are essential to a good diet, other than those in carbohydrates, fats, and proteins, provide no energy, but are required for other reasons. They may maintain or build strong bones and teeth, or they may help regulate the many chemical processes that take place in cells and body fluids.

Calcium (Ca), the major mineral found in bones and teeth, is needed for a variety of activities that go on in our cells. People who are growing require at least 1.2 g (1200 mg) of calcium per day because they are making new bone and tooth tissue. That's why young people are sometimes advised to drink lots of milk. Dairy products are a rich source of calcium, but dark green leafy vegetables, shellfish, citrus fruits, and legumes also contain calcium.

Phosphorus (P) is also essential for the growth of bones and teeth as well as for regulating chemical processes. A growing person's daily diet should contain at least 1 gram of phosphorus. Phosphorus is present in milk, dairy products, meat, fish, poultry, egg yolks, and whole-grain breads and cereals.

Iron (Fe) is an element found in hemoglobin, a protein in red blood cells. Hemoglobin combines with oxygen in the lungs and transports this vital element to all the cells of the body. Foods that contain iron include whole grains, egg yolk, beef (especially beef liver), shellfish, fruits, and green vegetables.

Iodine (I) is found in thyroxin, a hormone secreted by the thyroid gland that regulates the body's use of food. We need only about 0.000014 g of iodine per day to meet the needs of the thyroid gland.

Consequently, most water supplies contain all the iodine required in the daily diet. In regions where iodine is in short supply, the thyroid may enlarge, producing a swelling in the neck known as a goiter. The condition can be avoided by eating fish or using iodized salt.

Copper (Cu) is required for the manufacture of hemoglobin even though it is not an ingredient of the protein. This element is present in liver, nuts, legumes, fruits, and dark green leafy vegetables.

Zinc (Zn), which is found in whole grains, peas, fish, and lean meats, is needed for growth, tissue healing, and proper development of red blood cells.

To provide fluorine (F), which prevents tooth decay, many communities add fluoride salts to their water supply. The decline in tooth decay among children can be attributed to this practice and, some dentists believe, to the widespread use of fluoride treatments.

Sodium (Na), potassium (K), magnesium (Mg), chlorine (Cl), and trace quantities of a few more elements are also essential. They are involved in the processes that take place in and between muscle, nerve, blood, and other cells. These elements generally enter the body combined with other elements in compounds. For example, sodium and chlorine enter the body as ordinary salt, a compound chemically known as sodium chloride (NaCl).

VITAMINS

In 1912, Casimir Funk, a Polish chemist, suggested that many unexplained diseases such as beriberi, scurvy, and rickets were caused by a lack of certain unknown substances in the diet. He referred to these substances as *vitamines* because he thought they were amines (a type of chemical) essential to life. Later, the word was shortened to vitamins.

Vitamin B_1 was the first vitamin to be discovered. In 1897, Christiaan Eijkman, a Dutch physician, was in the East Indies trying to determine what germ caused beriberi. Beriberi is a disease that affects the nerves leading to and from the arms and legs. It causes loss of sensation and paralysis that is often followed by heart failure. Eijkman was unable to find any germ associated with beriberi. However, during his research there was a sudden outbreak of beriberi in the chickens he was using in his experiments. He found that these birds, that were being fed polished rice, were cured quickly when they ate unpolished (whole grain) rice.

A year later, an English biochemist, Frederick Hopkins, recognized that the disorder was a dietary deficiency. Something in the hull of the rice provided the necessary trace amount of what Funk later referred to as a vitamin. In 1926 the trace substance needed to prevent beriberi was isolated. It turned out to be a complex substance known as thiamine, which is found in such foods as whole grains (including rice), milk, liver, pork, and pasta. Since our daily requirement of thiamine is only 1.5 mg, deficiency of the vitamin is very rare.

Most vitamins cannot be made (synthesized) by the human body, but there are exceptions. Vitamin D can be produced in the body if sunlight reaches substances in the skin that can be made into vitamin D (calciferol). Vitamins B_{12} and K are synthesized by bacteria normally present in the intestine. But most vitamins are found in food. They are needed for growth and normal body activities.

Enzymes in the body catalyze (speed up) certain chemical reactions, such as the digestion of food. Vitamins are cofactors that help enzymes work. Without cofactors, which also serve as catalysts, the reactions would go much too slowly.

Vitamins A, D, E, and K are fat-soluble. That means that they dissolve in fats and will collect in fat cells in the body. Those vitamins can be harmful if taken in excess of body needs because they will accumulate in adipose (fat) tissue. Vitamins A and D are usually added to enrich lowfat milk because they are removed from whole milk along with the fat. The other vitamins are water-soluble. If large amounts of water-soluble vitamins are ingested, the excess is dissolved, carried away by body fluids, and excreted in the urine.

Vitamin B_2, riboflavin, is found in meat, especially liver, milk, eggs, dark green leafy vegetables, and whole grains. It is needed for the proper use of food and oxygen by the body. Lack of riboflavin causes severe skin problems, poor growth in children, nerve degeneration, and sensitivity to light. Since 1.7 mg of riboflavin meets our daily needs, few people in industrial nations suffer from lack of this vitamin.

Vitamin B_3, niacin, is present in whole grains, liver, fish, nuts, eggs, and legumes. It is essential in preventing pellagra, a disease that causes skin disorders, excessive salivation, diarrhea, vomiting, and mental confusion, including hallucinations. A normal diet that provides 20 mg or more of niacin is readily provided by the foods mentioned above. As a result, pellagra has been virtually eliminated from most industrial nations.

Pyridoxine (vitamin B_6), cobalamin (vitamin B_{12}), and folacin (folic acid), along with the other B vitamins, are all part of the vitamin B complex. Pyridoxine, found in whole grains, meats, spinach, green beans, and bananas, is necessary for the proper utilization of food by the body. Symptoms of its deficiency include nervousness, irritability, skin lesions, and, in children, convulsions.

Vitamin B_{12}, present in meat, fish, and milk products, is required for the manufacture of proteins and red blood cells. A deficiency can result in anemia (a low number of red blood cells), weakness, and intestinal disorders.

Folic acid (folacin) is required for the manufacture of nucleic acid, the utilization of protein, and the manufacture of red blood cells. It is present in liver, milk, eggs, fish, legumes, wheat germ, and cheese, but it can be destroyed by extensive cooking. Symptoms of its deficiency include anemia, weakness, and diarrhea. Recent studies by epidemiologist David Snowdon at the University of Kentucky suggest that Alzheimer's disease, which affects the brains of some elderly people, may be related to low levels of folic acid. His studies also indicate that subjects (nuns from the School Sisters of Notre Dame) with high levels of folic acid were less likely to exhibit the mental declines associated with Alzheimer's.

There is strong evidence of a link between a lack of folic acid and neural tube defects (spina bidifa and anencephaly) in fetuses. These defects develop in the early weeks of pregnancy, often before a woman knows she is pregnant. Because of this, the U.S. Food and Drug Administration (FDA) now requires that flours and many grain products (bread, cereal, rice, and noodles) be fortified with folic acid.

Vitamin C, ascorbic acid, is found in citrus fruits, tomatoes, green peppers, melons, and strawberries. We need at least 60 mg of this vitamin each day. Lack of vitamin C causes scurvy, a disease characterized by bleeding gums, loose teeth, and hemorrhaging into joints and muscles. These symptoms arise because ascorbic acid is required for the formation and maintenance of collagen, the connective tissue that holds cells together.

Early records of long sea voyages reveal that epidemics of scurvy often occurred aboard ships. British sailors came to be known as "limeys" because a physician in their navy discovered that lemons and limes in their diet prevented scurvy.

Nobel chemist Linus Pauling claimed that large doses of vitamin C could prevent the common cold. However, medical researchers have not been able to find evidence to support Pauling's claim. In fact, there is evidence that an excess of ascorbic acid can cause kidney stones and anemia due to the breakdown of red blood cells.

Vitamin A, retinol, is found in large amounts in fish-liver oils. However, any diet that includes vegetables and dairy products provides adequate quantities of vitamin A or a precursor of the vitamin. Carotene, an orange pigment present in vegetables such as carrots, can be changed into vitamin A in the body. The vitamin is needed for development of bones and teeth, maintenance of skin and membranes, and prevention of night blindness. Rod cells in the periphery of the eye contain visual purple, a substance that breaks down in the presence of light. Without vitamin A, visual purple cannot be synthesized. The result is an inability to convert light to the nervous impulses that allow us to see in dim light.

Vitamin D, calciferol, is needed to maintain the proper concentration of calcium and phosphorus in the blood, bones, and teeth. Lack of the vitamin can cause rickets, a disease associated with soft bones, which causes legs to bow and deformities to appear in the rib cage and skull. Vitamin D can be made if the body receives sufficient sunlight. It is also found in fish-liver oils, fortified milk, liver, and egg yolks.

Vitamin E, tocopherol, which is found in seed and vegetable oils and many other foods, is believed to be essential in maintaining the strength of cell membranes. It has been advocated for the treatment of a variety of body disorders.

Vitamin K, a complex organic chemical (methylphytylnaphthoquinone), is essential in the clotting of blood. A deficiency of vitamin K lowers the concentration of prothrombin, a substance involved in forming the clots that stop bleeding. The vitamin is present in a wide variety of vegetables, as well as egg yolks, liver, and fish oils.

Materials:

- an adult

- sensitive balance

- 0.25 gram of indophenol (2,6-dichloroindophenol, sodium salt)

- water

- measuring cup or graduated cylinder

- 2 pairs of rubber or plastic gloves

- 2 pairs of safety glasses

- clean 2-liter plastic soda bottle

- 500 milligram (0.5 g) of vitamin C

- paper

- hammer

- cup

- measuring teaspoon

- clear plastic vials or medicine cups

- eyedropper

- toothpicks

- notebook and pencil

- sink

- lemon

- lemon juice from concentrate

- pulp-free orange juice

- orange juice prepared from frozen concentrate

- canned orange juice

- grapefruit juice

- Kool-Aid

- Tang

- apple juice

- various reasonably clear juices that are not red or purple

- clear soda

You can test substances to see if they contain vitamin C (ascorbic acid) by using a chemical called indophenol. Its more technical name is sodium 2,6-dichloroindophenol, in case you have to buy some from a chemical supply company.

A freshly prepared solution of indophenol has a bluish color, but it turns colorless as vitamin C is added to it. You can compare the concentrations of vitamin C in different liquids by adding the liquids drop by drop to a fixed amount of indophenol solution. For example, suppose it takes only 2 drops of liquid X to turn 10 ml of an indophenol solution colorless. If it takes 6 drops of liquid Y to turn an identical sample of indophenol colorless, liquid Y contains about one third as much vitamin C as liquid X.

Ask an adult to help you prepare a solution of indophenol just before your experiment because indophenol deteriorates with time. **Indophenol powder should not touch your skin or eyes. Therefore, you should both wear gloves and safety glasses while preparing the solution.** The solution will be very dilute and far less harmful than the powder, so if any of the solution touches your skin simply rinse it off with water.

To prepare the indophenol solution that you will use, **have an adult** add 0.25 g of indophenol to 2.0 liters (2,000 ml) of water. (A clean 2-liter plastic soda bottle can hold all of the solution.) Stir or seal and shake to dissolve the solid. What is the percentage of indophenol in this solution? (Remember: 1.0 ml of water weighs 1.0 g.)

Next, crush 500 mg (0.5 g) of vitamin C. One 500-mg or two 250-mg vitamin C tablets will provide all the vitamin C you need. Place the tablet(s) on a piece of paper and strike the solid gently with a hammer. Press the particles with the hammer until you have a powder. Add the vitamin C powder to 100 ml of water in a cup. Stir until all the solid has dissolved. What is the percentage of vitamin C in this solution? You will use this solution as a standard vitamin C concentration. Other liquids that you test will be compared to this concentration of vitamin C.

Measure out 10 ml (2 tsp) of the indophenol solution and pour it into a clear plastic vial or a medicine cup. Pour 10 ml (2 tsp) of water into an identical vial or medicine cup. The water will serve as a control. Comparing the indophenol solution with the water will help you decide when the indophenol has become colorless.

Place the two vials or medicine cups side by side. Using an eyedropper, add 1 drop of the vitamin C solution to the indophenol. Then add 1 drop of the vitamin C solution to the vial or test tube that contains water. Use separate toothpicks to stir each solution. Has the vitamin C changed the color of the indophenol solution? Does the indophenol solution now match the color of the liquid in the vial of water? If not, continue to add the vitamin C solution 1 drop at a time to the indophenol and to the water. Do this until the bluish indophenol solution becomes colorless (not violet or pink, which may appear as an intermediate step) and has the same appearance as the vial or tube that contains plain water. Record the number of drops required to turn the indophenol colorless in your science notebook.

Rinse the vials or test tubes and the eyedropper thoroughly with water in a sink. Then repeat the test, but this time use the liquid obtained from a freshly squeezed lemon. How many drops of fresh lemon juice are required to turn the indophenol from blue to colorless? Record your results. How does the vitamin C content of the lemon juice compare with that of the vitamin C solution?

Repeat the test again using drops of lemon juice from concentrate. Record your results. How does the vitamin C content of the lemon juice from concentrate compare with that of the vitamin C solution? With that of the fresh lemon juice?

Use this experiment to test a number of other liquids for vitamin C. You might try pulp-free orange juice, orange juice prepared from a frozen concentrate, canned orange juice, grapefruit juice, Kool-Aid, Tang, apple juice, other juices that are reasonably clear, and a clear soda such as 7UP or Sprite. Which ones do you think will be good sources of vitamin C? After performing the tests, which ones do you conclude are good sources of vitamin C? Which are poor sources of vitamin C?

Make a list of the liquids you have tested in order of their vitamin C content starting with the highest concentration.

Science Fair Project Ideas

- Design and conduct an experiment to find out how leaving a vitamin C-rich liquid exposed to the air affects its concentration of vitamin C. Design and conduct another experiment to see how lack of refrigeration affects the vitamin C concentration of a vitamin C-rich liquid.
- Investigate how you might test for the presence of other vitamins.

Chapter 3

Yeast, Baking Soda, and Baking Powder

MANY FOODS THAT YOU AND YOUR FAMILY MEMBERS EAT HAVE PROBABLY BEEN PREPARED USING YEAST, BAKING SODA, OR BAKING POWDER. In this chapter you will learn why yeast is the baker's favorite organism and how that organism reacts with sugars. Most bread is made with a leavening agent, such as yeast, that causes fermentation (a change in form) and the production of carbon dioxide. (The word *leaven* comes from the Latin word *levare*, which means "to raise.") The empty spaces you find in bread make it light and fluffy. Those empty spaces were filled with carbon dioxide when the bread was baking.

Before the Egyptians discovered a way to make leavened bread about 4,500 years ago, all bread was heavier because it was unleavened. Unleavened bread is still made. For example, it is used in the Jewish festival of Passover.

You will also find out why baking soda or baking powder can replace yeast as a leavening agent in many recipes. You will discover, too, that baking soda has a myriad of uses, some of which have nothing to do with baking.

Materials:

- an adult
- masking tape
- marking pen
- one or more muffin tins
- granulated sugar
- syrup
- powdered sugar
- brown sugar
- diet sweetener
- flour
- cornstarch
- raw hamburger
- salt
- cooking oil
- milk
- dry yeast
- water
- measuring tablespoon

- measuring cup
- spoon
- measuring teaspoon (1 and ¼)
- toothpicks
- oven
- clock or watch
- limewater (or lime from a garden center)
- jar with lid
- clear vial
- drinking straw
- clay or one-hole stopper
- test tube
- glass tubing or flexible straw
- cooking oil
- plastic or rubber tubing

Yeasts are one-celled fungi. Like all fungi, they have no chlorophyll and, therefore, cannot manufacture their own food. Instead, they must absorb and digest organic matter. One commercially important food source for yeast is sugar. Yeasts obtain energy by converting sugar to alcohol and carbon dioxide. The chemical equation below represents this process. It shows that a sugar molecule consisting of 6 carbon atoms combined with 12 hydrogen atoms and 6 oxygen atoms, in the presence of yeast, is converted to 2 molecules of ethyl alcohol (C_2H_6O) and 2 molecules of carbon dioxide (CO_2).

$$C_6H_{12}O_6 + \text{yeast} \longrightarrow 2C_2H_6O + 2CO_2$$

Alcohol is the product sought by brewers, and carbon dioxide is the product that bakers use to make bread and other baked goods rise.

Glucose ($C_6H_{12}O_6$) is often obtained from sucrose ($C_{12}H_{22}O_{11}$), the white solid we use to sweeten our tea and cereal. Sucrose can be converted to glucose by enzymes in the cells of yeast (and by enzymes in our stomachs).

The carbon dioxide produced when yeast acts on sugar can be detected by the bubbles formed as carbon dioxide gas is released in the reaction. You can use the carbon dioxide bubbles to compare the effect of yeast on different foods.

To do this, first use masking tape and a marking pen to place the following labels next to the cups in one or more muffin tins: *control, granulated sugar, syrup, powdered sugar, brown sugar, diet sweetener, flour, cornstarch, raw hamburger, salt, cooking oil,* and *milk*. **Be sure to wash your hands with soap and warm water after touching raw meat.** Next, prepare a mixture of yeast and water by adding a tablespoon of dry yeast to a measuring cup that contains 250 ml (1 cup) of warm (35°C, or 95°F) water. Stir the mixture until it is uniform. Then add 1 tablespoon of this mixture to each of the 12 labeled muffin tin cups.

To the cup labeled *control*, add nothing more. It will serve as the control in this experiment. To the yeast-water mixture in the other 11 cups, add, as labeled, 1/4 teaspoon of one of the following: granulated sugar (sucrose), maple syrup, powdered sugar (sucrose), brown sugar, diet sweetener, flour, cornstarch, raw hamburger, salt, cooking oil, and milk. Stir the contents of each cup with a toothpick. In which ones do you see bubbles right away? Record your observations.

Under adult supervision, put the tin or tins in a warm (50°C, or 120°F) oven for about 10–15 minutes. Then check to see which samples show evidence of carbon dioxide bubbles. Place the tin(s) back in the warm oven and check for bubbles again after another 10–15 minutes. Record your observations each time. Does time have any effect on the production of carbon dioxide from the warm yeast-water-food mixtures? Which food or foods produced the most carbon dioxide when mixed with yeast and water?

What effect does the concentration of sugar have on the production of carbon dioxide? To find out, place a tablespoon of the yeast-water mixture in each of 5 muffin tin cups. Add 1/4 teaspoon of sugar to the first cup, 1/2 teaspoon to the second, 1 teaspoon to the third, and 2 teaspoons to the fourth. Add no sugar to the fifth cup; it will serve as a control. Label the cups, and put the muffin tin in a warm place. How does the concentration of sugar affect the production of carbon dioxide?

To see that the gas produced from the sugar-water-yeast mixture really is carbon dioxide, you can test it with limewater. Limewater turns milky in the presence of carbon dioxide. If you do not have any limewater, you can make some by obtaining lime from a garden or agricultural supply store. Just stir a teaspoon of the white solid into a small jar of water. Put a lid on the jar and let the mixture settle overnight. Carefully pour the liquid into a second jar, leaving any white solid behind. Then screw the lid on the jar.

To see the effect of carbon dioxide (CO_2) on limewater, pour a small volume of limewater into a clear vial. Then use a drinking straw and exhale gently into the limewater. Your exhalation contains about 4 percent CO_2. What happens to the limewater? **Do not drink the limewater.**

Prepare another yeast-water-sugar mixture by adding 1/2 teaspoon of yeast and an equal amount of sugar to a measuring cup that contains

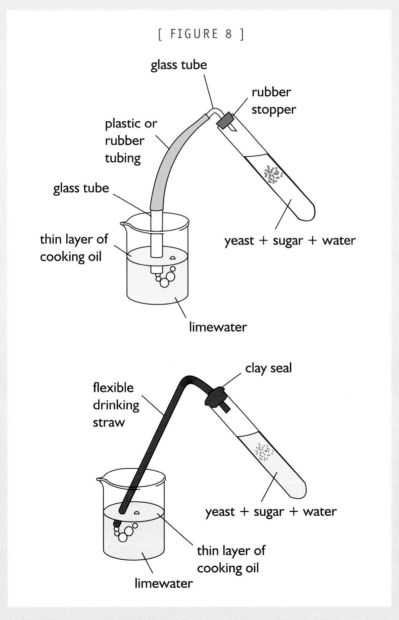

[FIGURE 8]

glass tube

rubber stopper

plastic or rubber tubing

glass tube

thin layer of cooking oil

yeast + sugar + water

limewater

clay seal

flexible drinking straw

yeast + sugar + water

thin layer of cooking oil

limewater

Limewater can be used to test for carbon dioxide. Either setup will work for this experiment.

50 ml of warm water (35°C, or 95°F). Stir the mixture until it is uniform. Add a small quantity of the mixture to a test tube. Place a one-hole rubber stopper with a short length of glass tubing into the tube's mouth. **Ask an adult to help you** insert the glass tubing into the rubber stopper. (A drop of cooking oil will serve to lubricate the glass and make insertion easier.) Attach a length of plastic or rubber tubing to the end of the glass tubing. It can carry any gas released by the yeast and sugar-water mixture to another piece of glass tubing immersed in a vial containing limewater covered with a thin layer of cooking oil (see Figure 8a). The oil will seal off the limewater from the air, which has a small concentration (0.04 percent) of CO_2. If you do not have a rubber stopper and glass tubing, you can use a flexible straw in place of the glass tube and clay in place of the stopper, as shown in Figure 8b.

🏆 Science Fair Project Idea

Design an experiment to find out how temperature affects the production of carbon dioxide from a yeast-water-sugar mixture. You can obtain a variety of temperatures by using a freezer, a refrigerator, a heated room, and an oven. What temperature provides the greatest production of carbon dioxide? What is the effect of extreme temperatures on the production of carbon dioxide? How can you explain this temperature effect?

Materials:
- dry yeast
- water
- measuring cup
- 3 juice glasses
- masking tape
- marking pen
- measuring tablespoon
- corn syrup
- granulated sugar
- cornstarch
- 3 spoons
- clock or watch
- notebook and pencil

For a closer look at how yeast reacts with different sugars, thoroughly mix a package of dry yeast with about 125 ml (1/2 cup) of warm (35°C, or 95°F) water. Pour about 1/3 of the mixture into each of 3 small juice glasses. Tape labels with the words *glucose*, *sucrose*, and *starch* to the glasses, as shown in Figure 9. Place the labeled glasses in a pan that is partially filled with warm (35°C, or 95°F) water. Add 1 tablespoon of corn syrup to the glass labeled *glucose*. (Corn syrup contains glucose sugar.) Add 1 tablespoon of ordinary granulated sugar to the cup labeled *sucrose*. Add 1 tablespoon of cornstarch to the remaining glass. Stir each mixture with a separate spoon.

Watch the mixtures over the next hour. In which glass do bubbles of carbon dioxide gas appear first? Place one ear near the top of each glass. Can you hear the gas bubbles fizzing and popping? In which container is gas produced at the fastest rate? In which glass do you first smell alcohol? In order to observe the bubbles of gas as they emerge from the mixture, you may have to use a spoon to remove the fine foam of bubbles that forms above the liquid. From the size and rate at which bubbles form, in which glass is the reaction proceeding fastest? Record your observations in your science notebook. Can you explain the results you observe?

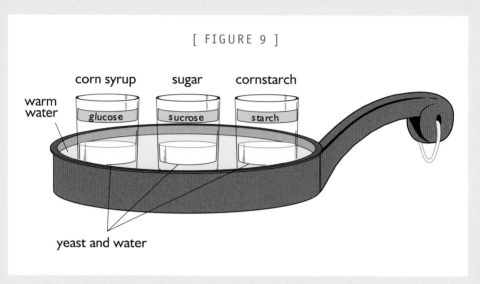

[FIGURE 9]

corn syrup   sugar   cornstarch

warm water

glucose   sucrose   starch

yeast and water

Yeast reacts with carbohydrates to form carbon dioxide and alcohol. Does it react faster with glucose, sucrose, or starch?

Science Fair Project Ideas

- Design an experiment to see what effect salt has on the reaction of yeast with sugar.
- Find a recipe for making bread that includes yeast and sugar. Make the bread. Then, **under adult supervision**, cut it open with a sharp knife. What evidence do you have that a gas was produced during the baking process?

3.3 Yeast as a Catalyst

Materials:

- an adult
- 3-percent solution of hydrogen peroxide (from a drugstore)
- measuring spoon or small graduated cylinder
- small test tube
- rusty nail
- boiling water
- coffee cup
- 12-oz Styrofoam cup
- alcohol thermometer ($-10-110°C$)
- matches
- candle
- thin piece of wood
- tablespoon
- dry yeast

Because this experiment involves flames and boiling water, you should work under adult supervision.

Yeast is sometimes used with substances other than foods because it can act as a catalyst. A catalyst is a substance that changes the speed of a chemical reaction without being chemically changed by the reaction. Catalysts are widely used in food processing and in the production of many products used in your home. Hydrogen peroxide (H_2O_2) is a chemical that changes slowly into water and oxygen. The reaction can be represented by the following chemical equation:

$$2H_2O_2 \longrightarrow 2H_2O + O_2$$

As you probably know, oxygen is a gas that supports combustion. That is, substances such as wood, coal, alcohol, and many other things burn if oxygen is present. Because air is 21 percent oxygen, those substances burn in air. However, they burn much faster in pure oxygen.

The rate at which hydrogen peroxide breaks down into water and oxygen can be greatly increased by adding a catalyst. To see the effect of a catalyst, pour 5 ml (1 tsp) of a 3-percent solution of hydrogen peroxide into a small test tube. Do you see any evidence, such as the formation of bubbles, of a gas being released?

Place a rusty nail in the liquid and watch it closely for a few minutes. Rust is iron oxide, which can sometimes act as a catalyst. Can you see bubbles of gas collecting on the nail?

Under adult supervision, pour some boiling water into a coffee cup. Place the test tube in the hot water and observe the peroxide and nail for a few minutes. Does temperature have any effect on the rate at which the liquid decomposes?

To find out if yeast will catalyze the reaction, add about 60 ml (2 oz) of a 3-percent solution of hydrogen peroxide to a 12-oz Styrofoam cup. Place a thermometer in the liquid and measure its temperature. While waiting for the thermometer to reach a steady reading, **have an adult help you** light a candle and prepare a thin piece of wood about 10 cm (4 in) long that you can use as a glowing splint.

Record the temperature of the hydrogen peroxide solution and remove the thermometer. Then pour a tablespoon of dry yeast into the solution. What happens?

Under adult supervision, prepare a glowing splint by placing one end of the thin piece of wood in the candle flame. Let it burn for a few seconds, then blow it out. The splint should be glowing but not burning when you place it in the bubbles of gas forming in the Styrofoam cup, as shown in Figure 10. What happens to the glowing splint? What evidence do you have that oxygen is being produced?

Put the thermometer back in the liquid. What has happened to the temperature of the liquid?

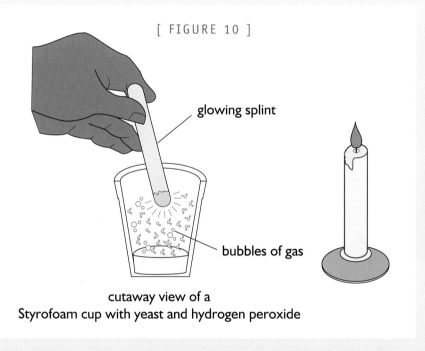

[FIGURE 10]

glowing splint

bubbles of gas

cutaway view of a
Styrofoam cup with yeast and hydrogen peroxide

What happens when a glowing splint is placed in the bubbles of gas
that form when yeast is added to hydrogen peroxide?

Reactions that produce heat cause an increase in temperature and are called *exothermic* reactions. Those that absorb heat show a decrease in temperature and are called *endothermic* reactions. Is the decomposition of hydrogen peroxide an exothermic or an endothermic reaction? What makes you think so?

Science Fair Project Idea

Carry out an investigation of catalysts. How are they used in the food industry? What other household products require catalysts? What catalysts are found in your body and why are they important?

Materials:

-an adult
-baking soda
-measuring teaspoon
-widemouthed glass,
 jar, or beaker
-eyedropper
-vinegar
-clay
-birthday candle

-matches
-lemon juice
-orange juice
-pickle juice
-Tang crystals
-Kool-Aid crystals
-water
-can of baking
 powder

Yeast is not the only ingredient that can be used to produce a gas and make breads and cakes less dense and more appetizing. Baking soda can also be used to produce carbon dioxide. Baking soda, as you can see from the list of ingredients on its box, is 100 percent sodium bicarbonate ($NaHCO_3$).

To see how baking soda can be used to make carbon dioxide, pour 1 teaspoon of the powder into a widemouthed glass, jar, or beaker. Then add a few drops of vinegar. What happens?

To see that the gas produced is probably carbon dioxide, which does not burn and will, in fact, smother a fire, repeat the experiment. This time, though, use a small piece of clay to support a birthday candle on the bottom of the vessel, as shown in Figure 11. **With an adult present**, light the candle before you add the vinegar. What happens to the candle flame as the gas produced by the reaction surrounds it?

What evidence do you have to support the idea that carbon dioxide is produced when vinegar is added to baking soda? What could you do to be more certain that the gas is carbon dioxide?

[FIGURE 11]

vinegar

baking soda

Use a candle flame to find out what gas is produced when baking soda and vinegar are mixed.

Will any acid react with baking soda to produce the gas? To find out, try adding lemon juice, orange juice, and pickle juice to separate samples of baking soda. Do these acids react with baking soda to form a gas? Which liquid appears to be the strongest acid? Which appears to be the weakest acid? What makes you think so?

Some solids such as Tang and Kool-Aid crystals have acidic properties when dissolved in water. To see whether these substances will react with baking soda in the same way as vinegar, mix each of these solids with a little baking soda in separate containers. Then add a few drops of water. What do you observe?

As you know, baking soda is sodium bicarbonate. Look at the list of ingredients on a can of baking *powder*. It contains sodium bicarbonate, cornstarch, and a solid acid such as calcium dihydrogen phosphate $[Ca(H_2PO_4)_2]$. Predict what will happen if you add water to a teaspoon of baking powder, then try it. Was your prediction correct? Why do many baking recipes call for baking powder?

Science Fair Project Ideas

- Some baking recipes include baking soda rather than baking powder or yeast but no solid acid. In all these recipes, the dough is heated. Could it be that baking soda breaks down and releases carbon dioxide when heated? Design an experiment to find out. Then carry out your experiment **under adult supervision**.

- Examine a cookbook. Look for recipes that call for baking soda. Try one of the recipes and see if you can predict what will happen when the ingredients are heated.

- Baking soda is sometimes thrown onto small fires. Why would anyone add baking soda to a fire?

Materials:

- an adult
- safety goggles
- large plastic jar with a screw-on lid
- small, tall jar such as an olive jar
- hammer
- nail
- smooth board
- graduated cylinder or measuring cup
- water
- measuring tablespoon
- vinegar
- sink
- soda-acid fire extinguisher (if available)
- box of baking soda (16-oz)
- cornstarch
- cooking pan
- cooking oil
- stove
- old dinner plate
- cloth
- marking pens or watercolors

In addition to its use in baking, sodium bicarbonate has a variety of purposes. It is used to make other chemicals. It is found in many medicines, such as antacids. Because it is a weak base, it can be mixed with water and drunk to relieve acid indigestion. It can be used to soak feet. It can be used to clean teeth, shower stalls, tiles, cutting boards, steel knives, combs, and hair brushes. It is also used to absorb odors from refrigerators, clothes hampers, and pet cages. It can soften bathwater, clean silver, polish chrome, remove corrosion from car batteries, and soften the quills for easier removal from a dog that was too successful in chasing a porcupine. Because it decomposes when heated to form carbon dioxide, it is often spread on oil fires to smother the flames.

A BAKING SODA FIRE EXTINGUISHER

Another use of baking soda is in fire extinguishers. As you know from the previous experiment, baking soda, when mixed with an acid, produces carbon dioxide, a gas that can be used to smother fires. To see how such a fire extinguisher works, make one from a large plastic jar that has a screw-on lid and a small, tall jar such as an olive jar.

Remove the lid from the large jar and, **wearing safety goggles**, use a hammer and nail to punch a small hole through the lid, as shown in Figure 12a. Pour about 500 ml (2 cups) of water into the jar. Add about 2 tablespoons of baking soda and stir the mixture. Be sure the mouth of the smaller empty bottle will be above the level of the solution in the large jar when it is placed in the jar. If this is not the case, pour some of the solution out of the jar.

Nearly fill the smaller bottle with vinegar. Carefully place this bottle on the bottom of the large jar, as shown in Figure 12b. Screw the lid with the hole back onto the large jar. Hold the jar next to a sink. Then turn it on its side and point it down into the sink. What happens? How can you explain what you observe?

Read the instructions on a soda-acid fire extinguisher and the ingredients, if listed. After reading, explain how this kind of fire extinguisher works.

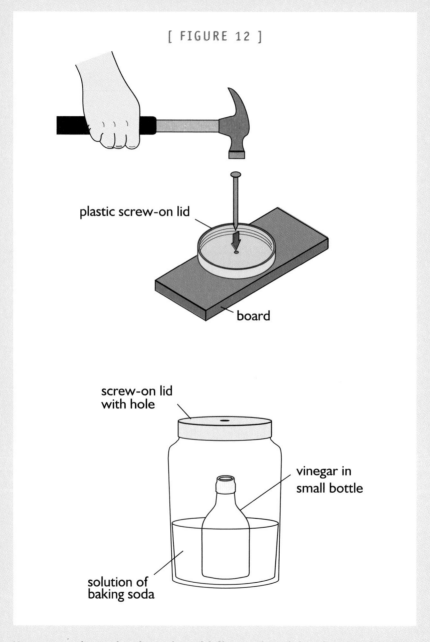

[FIGURE 12]

plastic screw-on lid

board

screw-on lid
with hole

vinegar in
small bottle

solution of
baking soda

You can make a simple soda-acid fire extinguisher in your kitchen.

BAKING SODA CLAY

You can make your own clay from baking soda. Mix together a 16-oz box of baking soda and a cup of cornstarch in a cooking pan. Then add about 300 ml (1 1/4 cups) of water and a tablespoon of cooking oil. **Under adult supervision**, stir this mixture as you heat it slowly on a stove for about 15 minutes or until it reaches a uniform and moderately thick consistency.

Pour the warm mixture onto an old dinner plate and cover with a damp cloth. After the mixture has cooled, spread cornstarch on a smooth board, place the mixture on the board, and knead the clay as you would dough until it is smooth. You can use the clay to mold and sculpt a variety of creations. Let the clay dry and then color or paint with marking pens or watercolors.

 Science Fair Project Ideas

- Look at a variety of containers that hold foods and other materials in your kitchen and bathroom. Check the list of ingredients on these containers. How many contain sodium bicarbonate (baking soda)?
- Find out where sodium bicarbonate comes from and what industrial uses it serves.
- What is the difference between sodium bicarbonate and sodium carbonate (soda)? Can one be obtained from the other?

Dairy products include milk, cheese, butter, and yogurt.

Chapter 4

Dairy Products

YOU PROBABLY DRINK MILK AND EAT OTHER DAIRY PRODUCTS EVERY DAY. This chapter will allow you to learn more about milk, cheese, butter, margarine, mayonnaise, and ice cream.

Have you ever added salt to a glass of water and stirred it? If so, you made a solution. Solutes (like the salt) dissolve in a solvent (water) to produce a solution. In a solution, the pieces of solutes become so small that you can see them only with a very powerful microscope. Because the solutes are so small, the solution becomes clear and transparent. But not all substances dissolve in a solvent to produce a solution. In some cases, a substance does not completely dissolve to become invisible. Instead, the substance forms particles that are larger than those found in solutions. Although they are quite small, these particles remain large enough to be evenly suspended or spread throughout the liquid. Whenever two substances are mixed so that one becomes suspended, but not dissolved, in the other, a colloid has been prepared. A colloid contains small particles that remain suspended in a substance, which is usually a liquid.

Examples of colloids you can eat include butter, whipped cream, gelatin desserts, mustard, jelly, and ketchup. In each of these, substances are broken down into particles that are suspended in a liquid. For example, butter consists of water particles that are suspended in liquid fats.

Whipped cream is made by suspending the gas particles present in air in heavy cream. Ketchup is prepared by crushing tomatoes, sugar, and spices and then suspending them in water and vinegar.

The particles suspended in a colloid can be brought closer together. If enough particles are clumped together, either the colloid turns into a solid or a solid mass of material forms within the colloid. Whenever you prepare a gelatin dessert, you begin by suspending the powdered materials in water to form a colloid. Refrigerating the colloid causes the particles to come together, turning the colloid into a solid that can be eaten. How could you change the solid back into a colloid?

Materials:
- an adult
- buttermilk
- regular milk
- small pot
- stove
- large plastic container
- spoon
- measuring cup
- alcohol thermometer (-10–110° C)
- cheesecloth
- rennin tablet (Junket Rennet Tablets are available in supermarkets.)

In addition to changing the temperature, another way to clump the particles in a colloid is to add certain chemicals. You can check this out in an experiment using milk, which is another example of a colloid. One of the solutes in milk is a sugar called lactose. Some people cannot digest, or break down, the lactose. As a result the lactose remains in their digestive tract where it can cause cramps, bloating, and diarrhea. To avoid these problems, people with this condition must drink lactose-free milk. Unlike regular milk, lactose-free milk will never turn sour. Given enough time, the lactose in regular milk turns into another chemical called lactic acid, which has a sour taste.

You can always tell if milk is sour by tasting it. But you really do not want to do that. Fortunately there is a more pleasant way. Just look for clumps in the milk. These clumps are all the particles, including lactic acid, that come together when milk sours. Both cheese and cream cheese are made by first clumping all the particles in milk. Here is how to make your own cheese.

[FIGURE 13]

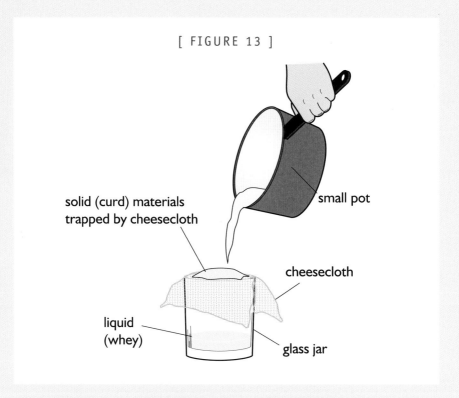

solid (curd) materials
trapped by cheesecloth

small pot

cheesecloth

liquid
(whey)

glass jar

**Cheesecloth is very useful for separating solid material from a liquid.
Just be sure to pour the mixture through the cheesecloth slowly.**

Add about 1 fluid ounce of buttermilk to about 200 fluid ounces of regular milk in a plastic container. Stir to mix the buttermilk and the milk. The buttermilk contains a chemical that causes the lactose to turn into lactic acid rather quickly. But it does take some time, so allow the container to stand for at least four hours. While you are waiting, you can use the leftover buttermilk to make pancakes.

Pour the milk sample into a pot. **Under adult supervision**, gently warm the milk to around 30°C (86°F). While stirring, add a crushed rennin tablet to the milk. Rennin is sold in supermarkets under the trade name Junket Rennet Tablets. Slowly increase the temperature of the milk to 38°C (100°F). Do not allow the temperature to go any higher. Continue stirring and heating for several minutes.

Examine the contents of your pot. If you wish, you can collect the clumped particles (your cheese!) by filtering the contents of the pot through cheesecloth, as shown in Figure 13. Can you guess how cheese-cloth got its name? Allow the solids to dry. The solids are known as the curd, and the liquid that passed through the cheesecloth is called the whey. Add some salt and taste your cheese. Unfortunately, it will not taste anything like the cheese you find at the supermarket. Commercial cheese is prepared in a more elaborate manner and is slowly aged to give it flavor and texture. Do not try aging yours because it will probably spoil. Cheese makers add chemicals to prevent spoiling.

Science Fair Project Ideas

- Adding vinegar to milk and then heating it produces a gluelike substance. Pour 125 ml of nonfat milk and 25 ml of vinegar into a small pot. **Under adult supervision**, heat the mixture gently while stirring continuously until small lumps begin to form. Remove the pot from the stove and continue to stir until no more lumps form. Allow the lumps to settle and then filter the mixture through cheesecloth to collect the curds. Return the solid to the pot. Add 30 ml of water to the solid and stir. Add 1/2 teaspoon of baking soda. Observe what happens. Continue to add a little more baking soda until no more bubbles appear. Scrape out the solid material from the pot and test its adhesive properties.

- Try to develop the most adhesive glue by varying the proportions of the ingredients. Compare the properties of your product to commercial glues. You can test their adhesive properties on paper, wood, and metal objects. If your product glues two things together, how well does it work compared to commercial products? You might measure drying time or holding strength. Do research to learn more about the chemistry of glue making.

BUTTER AND MARGARINE

You have probably heard that fat is bad for you. Actually, fats are an essential part of nutrition. They are an important energy source, and they are needed to make cell membranes and hormones in the body. Certain types of fat or high levels of fat in your diet, however, can be unhealthy. Most animal fats are saturated fats (lard and butter) and are solid at room temperature. Diets high in saturated fats have been shown to contribute to high cholesterol, which is linked to cardiovascular disease. Saturated fats cause deposits of fat to build up in blood vessels, reduce blood flow, and stress the heart. Fats from fish and plants are unsaturated fats called oils. Usually liquid at room temperature, unsaturated fats may actually reduce the risk of cardiovascular diseases.

Because of the negative health effects of eating lots of saturated fats like butter, butter-substitutes, and margarine are widely produced and sold. Some people believe that margarine is a healthier choice than butter because it is produced from plant fats. However, the manufacture of margarine may convert unsaturated fats to saturated fats or trans fats by adding hydrogen. The result is called "hydrogenated vegetable oil." (You may have noticed those words on the food labels of snacks that you eat). Trans fats are even worse for your health than saturated fats.

To understand the difference between an animal fat and a vegetable oil, you need to take a brief look at some chemistry.

Both fats and oils are organic compounds. You may be familiar with the word *organic* from having heard the phrases "organically grown" or "contains only natural, organic ingredients." In chemistry, the word *organic* has a different meaning. An organic compound is defined as any chemical substance that contains the element carbon. You can think of an element as the building block of a chemical compound. In addition to carbon, fats and oils also contain the elements oxygen and hydrogen.

$$H - \underset{\underset{H}{\overset{\overset{H}{|}}{|}}{C}} - \underset{\underset{H}{\overset{\overset{H}{|}}{|}}{C}} - \underset{\underset{H}{\overset{\overset{H}{|}}{|}}{C}} - C \overset{O}{\underset{OH}{}}$$

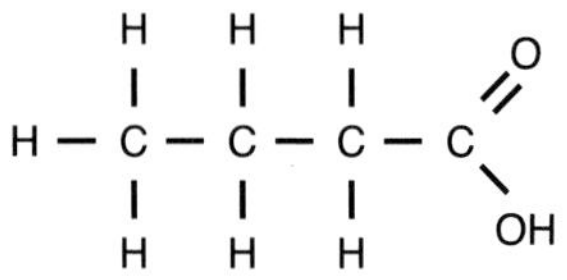

[FIGURE 14b]

$$H - C - C - C = C - C - C = C - C - C = C - C - C - C - C - C - C - C - C \overset{O}{\underset{OH}{}}$$

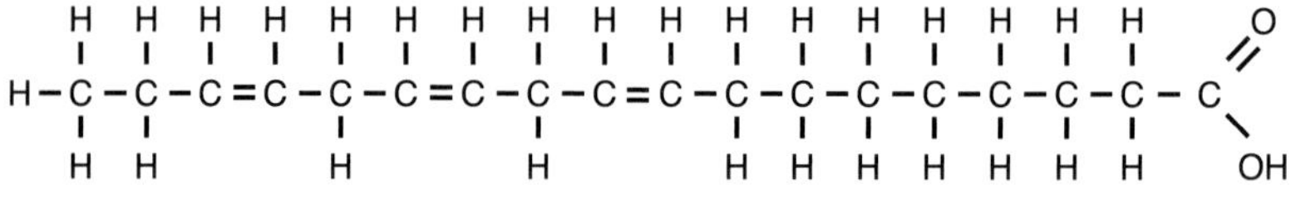

Both these compounds are known as fatty acids. Notice that both these compounds have a −COOH (carboxyl) group of atoms at the end. Locate this group. This group makes these compounds fatty acids.

BUTTER AND MARGARINE ARE LIPIDS

Fats and oils are classified as lipids. A lipid is an organic compound that has many more carbon and hydrogen atoms than oxygen atoms. For example, examine the following chemical formula for a lipid: $C_{57}H_{110}O_6$. A chemical formula is a shorthand method for providing some information about a chemical compound. The formula for the fat tells you that there are 57 carbon atoms, 110 hydrogen atoms, and only 6 oxygen atoms in this compound. An atom is the smallest unit of an element.

A chemical formula does not provide enough information to show the important difference between animal fats and vegetable oils. In order to understand this difference, you must examine another type of formula called a *structural formula*. A structural formula shows the arrangement of all the atoms of the various elements in a compound. For example, Figure 14a shows the structural formula for a compound found in butter. Compare this structural formula to the one shown in Figure 14b, which shows a compound found in vegetable oil. What similarities do you notice? What differences do you see?

If you examine the lines connecting several of the carbon atoms in the vegetable oil, you will see double lines in three places. There are no double lines between the carbon atoms in the animal oil. Those lines, whether single or double, represent chemical bonds. A chemical bond joins one atom to another. Whenever a fat contains one or more double bonds that connect carbon atoms, it is said to be unsaturated. What is a polyunsaturated fat? If all the bonds are single ones, the fat is said to be saturated.

QUALITATIVE OBSERVATIONS VERSUS QUANTITATIVE OBSERVATIONS

You can easily determine if a food contains either unsaturated or saturated fats. To test a food sample for fat, just rub some of it on a brown paper bag. Look for any grease stains that appear. In this case, you are making a qualitative observation. A qualitative observation involves simply noting whether some characteristic is present or absent. By looking for a grease stain, you are simply determining whether a food sample contains or does not contain fat. But scientists often make quantitative observations. A quantitative observation involves determining numerical information, for example, the amount of fat in a food sample. Your experiments in determining the mineral and protein content of milk involved quantitative observations. In Experiment 4.2, you will make quantitative observations about fat.

Materials:
- science teacher
- safety goggles
- several different vegetable oils
- iodine crystals
- hexane
- science lab ventilating hood
- balance accurate to 0.01 g
- eyedropper
- graduated cylinder or pipettes
- test tubes
- beaker

Unsaturated fats react with iodine. As Figure 15 shows, a double bond can be broken, making room for iodine atoms. The more double bonds present, the more that can be broken, and the more iodine that can be added until all the double bonds have been changed into single ones. At that point, any additional iodine that is added to the saturated compound does not react with the oil but remains in solution. Thus the solution turns violet at this point. Iodine cannot be added to a saturated fat because there are no double bonds that can be broken. Thus, just a drop or two of iodine to a saturated fat causes the solution to turn violet.

You can test various vegetable oils to see which is the most unsaturated. **You must work with a physical science or chemistry teacher** to use the equipment and materials needed for this experiment. You need a balance accurate enough to weigh 0.05 g of iodine crystals. You also need a solvent that will dissolve iodine crystals. Water is not a good choice in this case. Because fats and water do not mix, you must use a solvent that

[FIGURE 15]

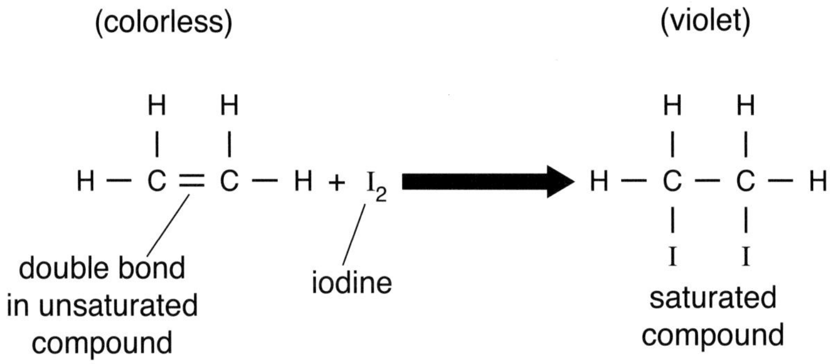

Notice where the iodine atoms can be added to an unsaturated fat. Once all the double bonds are broken, then the compound is said to be "saturated" because it cannot hold any more atoms.

will dissolve the iodine crystals and then mix with the oils. Such a solvent must be a nonpolar, organic solvent.

You know what organic means, but what is the difference between nonpolar and polar? Simply stated, a polar compound has regions with different electric charges. In the case of water, one end of the compound has a negative charge, while the other end has a positive charge. A nonpolar compound does not have regions with different electric charges. Instead, different regions of the compound have the same charge, or the charge is evenly distributed. Oils are nonpolar compounds and can be dissolved only in nonpolar solvents. A phrase that is used in chemistry is "like dissolves like."

Care must be used when selecting a nonpolar, organic solvent to dissolve fats. Perhaps the safest nonpolar, organic compound to use is hexane. Be sure to use a ventilating hood **under your teacher's supervision** when using hexane. Also be sure to **wear safety goggles.** Dissolve 0.05 g of iodine crystals in a beaker of 100 ml of hexane. In a test tube, mix 5 ml of hexane with 5 ml of the oil being tested, and then add the iodine solution a drop at a time. You can test various vegetable oils, including olive, peanut, sunflower, walnut, corn, coconut, and canola oils. Count the number of drops of iodine needed to turn the oil-hexane mixture violet.

Set up a table showing your results in degrees of unsaturation. Your table will be based on the oil that requires the fewest drops before turning violet. Use this oil as the basis for calculating the degree of unsaturation of the other oils. For example, if another oil takes twice as many iodine drops, then this oil is twice as unsaturated.

MAKING MARGARINE AND BUTTER

If margarine contains vegetable oil, then how can it be a solid? The answer can be found in the process that is used to make margarine. Margarine is made using a procedure similar to the one you used when you added iodine to break the double bonds in the unsaturated fats in oil. In the case of margarine, the procedure is called *hydrogenation*. That means that a double bond between 2 carbon atoms in the unsaturated fat is broken and 2 hydrogen atoms are added, as shown in Figure 16.

The double bonds make the unsaturated fat a liquid (oil) at room temperature. By adding hydrogen, some of the double bonds are changed to single bonds. When a certain number of double bonds have been changed into single bonds, the liquid oil becomes a solid. In other words, margarine is nothing more than a hydrogenated vegetable oil. Tell someone that the next time they spread margarine on toast or put it on a baked potato.

You may find a hydrogenated vegetable oil not only in your refrigerator but also in a kitchen cabinet. Hydrogenated vegetable oil is the main ingredient in a product known as solid shortening. Mix 2 tablespoons of water with 1 cup of shortening and you have margarine. It will not taste like the real thing because the margarine in your refrigerator contains salt, artificial color, and artificial flavors to improve its taste and appearance. In fact, the margarine you make from shortening may taste more like the margarine that first appeared in stores in the late 1800s. Concerned about the possible loss of business when margarine first appeared, butter manufacturers pressured politicians into passing laws that required margarine to be both unappetizing and unappealing. The margarine first sold in stores did not taste great and had a very unpleasant brown color.

[FIGURE 16]

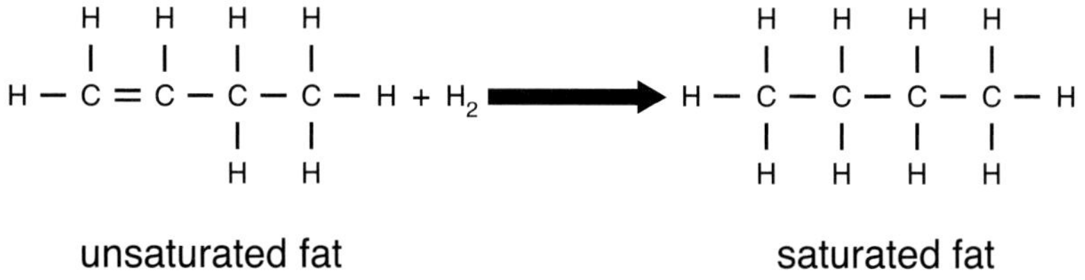

unsaturated fat   saturated fat

An unsaturated fat can be turned into a saturated fat by breaking the double bond and adding hydrogen atoms.

Science Fair Project Idea

Many people are concerned about their diets. Some people avoid eating fats. Yet, everyone needs some fat as a part of his or her regular diet to stay healthy. Search the library and the Internet for information on diets. How do they compare in terms of their fat recommendations and total calorie intake? Look especially for information concerning any long-term studies. For example, which diets, if any, claim to be successful in maintaining a weight loss 2 or 3 years after a person starts the program? Also check for information about substances known as trans fatty acids, which are present in margarine. How do they affect diet recommendations? Summarize all your findings in a written report.

4.3 What Is the Mineral Content of Milk?

Rather than clump all the solutes in milk at once, you can isolate each type of solute and determine how much of it is present. For example, you can determine the mineral and protein content of milk. The minerals include calcium, magnesium, zinc, phosphorus, and iron, all of which are needed for good health. Those minerals are dissolved in milk. The proteins are much larger and, therefore, are suspended, rather than dissolved, in the milk. Like the minerals, the proteins can be easily separated from everything else that is in milk.

Weigh a measuring cup on a kitchen scale. Pour a small amount of milk into the measuring cup and weigh it again. Calculate the mass of the milk by subtracting the mass of the measuring cup from the mass of the measuring cup and milk. Pour some water into a pot. Cover the pot with heavy-duty aluminum foil, making a depression in the middle. Using a nail, punch small holes through the foil near the inside rim of the pot, as shown in Figure 17. Remove the foil, weigh it, and then replace it on the pot. Carefully pour the milk into the depression.

Under adult supervision, gently heat the milk on a stove to evaporate the water (the solvent) in the milk. Continue heating until all that remains on the aluminum foil are brownish-black ashes. Be sure that there is always enough water in the pot. If you must add more water, turn off the heat and wait until the pot has cooled. Then carefully lift the foil and pour more water into the pot. Continue heating until only ashes remain. Allow everything to cool and remove the foil, making sure not to lose any ashes. Weigh the foil and ashes.

[FIGURE 17]

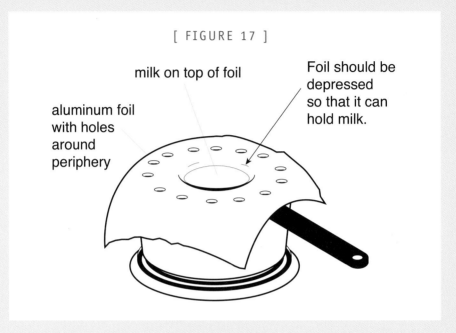

milk on top of foil

Foil should be depressed so that it can hold milk.

aluminum foil with holes around periphery

Heat from the stove will evaporate most of the solvent in milk, leaving the minerals in the aluminum foil. Why should you punch small holes in the aluminum foil before heating the water in the pot?

The ashes represent the minerals that remain after evaporating the water and other combustible substances in milk. (A combustible substance is one that will burn.) Calculate the mineral content of the milk by placing your data in the following equation:

$$\frac{\text{mass of ash}}{\text{mass of milk}} \times 100 = \text{percent mineral content}$$

Materials:
- egg
- measuring spoons
- vinegar
- salt
- mustard
- salad oil
- blender
- measuring cup
- lemon juice

Have you ever tried to mix oil and vinegar to make a salad dressing? No matter how hard you shake the two liquids, once you stop, the oil collects as tiny drops that eventually come together and separate from the vinegar. Obviously oil does not form either a solution or colloid with vinegar. However, if another substance is added, then the oil and vinegar will not separate. Instead they will remain mixed so that one liquid remains distributed as small drops in the other liquid. Whenever two liquids are prepared in this way, an emulsion has been made. The substance that is added to make the emulsion is called an *emulsifier*. Figure 18 shows how an emulsifier acts as a bridge between two liquids that normally do not mix. Eggs are good emulsifiers. You can see for yourself by using an egg to make mayonnaise.

Mix 1 egg, 1 tablespoon of vinegar, 1/2 teaspoon of salt, 1/2 teaspoon of mustard, and 1/4 cup of salad oil in a blender. Blend this mixture for several seconds. Add 3/4 cup of salad oil to the mixture in a slow, steady stream while blending, until most of the oil is absorbed to form an emulsion. This is your mayonnaise.

Experiment with ways of making mayonnaise by varying the proportions or testing different ingredients. For example, substitute lemon juice in place of vinegar. Check a cookbook on how to use an emulsifier to make Hollandaise sauce. Who knows—this may be the start of your career as one of the great chefs or food scientists of the world, if not your neighborhood.

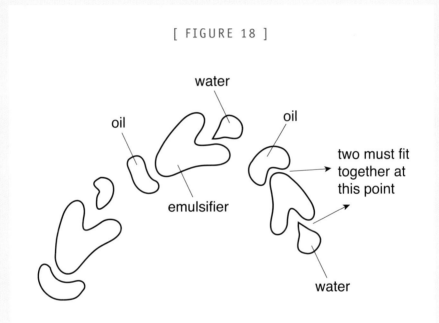

[FIGURE 18]

water

oil

oil

two must fit
together at
this point

emulsifier

water

An emulsifier can be used to mix two substances that normally do not
mix. One end of an emulsifier molecule attracts one substance, such
as water. The other end of the emulsifier attracts the other substance,
such as oil, bringing the two substances together.

Chapter 5

Fruits, Vegetables, Gelatin, Meat, and Carbonated Drinks

THE PREVIOUS CHAPTERS OF THIS BOOK PROVIDED YOU WITH AN OPPORTUNITY TO LEARN ABOUT AND TEST FOR CARBOHYDRATES, FATS, PROTEINS, VITAMINS, AND MINERALS. You investigated how yeast, baking soda, and baking powder are used in baking many things that you eat. You learned how to make cheese, butter, margarine, and mayonnaise. This final chapter offers some additional experiments that you may find fun. You will be introduced to some ways foods are kept fresh or processed. You will experiment with things that you eat or drink on a regular basis. You may be surprised to find that reactions take place between certain foods.

In the first few experiments, you will work with fruits and vegetables. You have probably heard that eating a variety of brightly colored fruits and vegetables is healthy. They are brightly colored because they contain chemicals known as pigments. Fruits and vegetables also contain carbohydrates, vitamins, antioxidants, and even enzymes.

The next few experiments use meat tenderizer and meat. The many different types of meat readily available include beef, chicken, pork, veal, and lamb.

The final few experiments deal with carbonated beverages. If you look on a can or bottle of any carbonated drink, the first ingredient listed is carbonated water. Carbonated water is water that contains dissolved carbon dioxide (CO_2). The trapped CO_2 gas causes bubbles to form when a bottle or can is opened. Dissolved CO_2 also gives water a taste that is sometimes described as "sharp" or "acidic."

Materials:

-an adult
-large drinking glass
-knife
-orange juice
-apple
-clock or watch
-2 plates
-water
-other kinds of juice
-other kinds of fruit

Fruit juices are solutions that contain various solutes dissolved in water. For example, orange juice contains several solutes, including sugars, minerals, and vitamins, especially vitamin C. Vitamin C has a chemical name—ascorbic acid. Without vitamin C, your body could not stay intact. The soft tissues in your joints and gums would start to fall apart, causing bleeding. Injured tissue would not be able to repair itself.

Because your body cannot make vitamin C, you must get it from foods and beverages. Which products shown in Figure 19 contain vitamin C? Many people also take vitamin C tablets. Besides being required for good health, vitamin C can also be used to keep foods fresh. In other words, vitamin C can be used as a preservative. Here is your chance to see what you can keep fresh with vitamin C.

Under adult supervision cut an apple into bite-sized slices. Soak half the slices in orange juice. After soaking them for 30 minutes, remove the apple slices and rinse them with water. Place those soaked in orange juice on one plate. Place those that were not soaked in orange juice on a second plate. Compare what happens to the apples on each plate. Which ones turn brown sooner? You should now realize why chefs sometimes squeeze a lemon or lime over a Waldorf salad, which contains freshly cut apples.

[FIGURE 19]

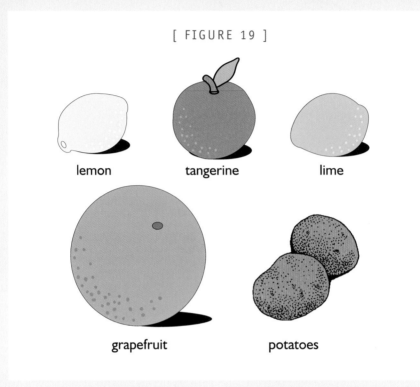

lemon tangerine lime

grapefruit potatoes

All these supermarket items contain vitamin C. However, the citrus fruits here are rich in vitamin C compared with the potatoes.

By the way, here is your chance to really "play" with your food and friends at the same time! Invite your friends to your home and ask each one to bring a different brand of juice or a different piece of fruit. Experiment to see which type of juice—orange, lemon, lime, grapefruit, cranberry, grape, or pineapple—works best as a preservative. Which type of fruit—pear, banana, peach, or kiwi—is preserved the best? Which combination of fruit juice and fruit works best?

Materials:
- 2 celery stalks
- 2 glasses
- water
- refrigerator

Have you ever noticed a sprinkler system come on in the vegetable section of a supermarket? Periodically, the system comes on and sprays the produce with water. If the vegetables were not kept moist, people might not buy them because they would not look fresh. Without enough water, vegetables wilt because of a lack of turgor pressure.

Turgor pressure is the pressure that water exerts inside a plant cell. As you can see in Figure 20, a plant cell is surrounded by two structures. One structure is called a *cell membrane*. The second structure surrounds the cell membrane and is known as a *cell wall*. Both plant and animal cells have cell membranes, but only plant cells have a cell wall. Unlike a cell membrane, a cell wall is rigid. As water moves into a plant cell, it pushes the cell membrane against the cell wall, creating the force of turgor pressure that keeps the cell walls stiff and the plants crisp.

Place one stalk of celery in a glass and the other stalk in a glass half filled with water. Refrigerate both glasses and observe what happens to the celery stalks over the next several days. Which one would you buy in a supermarket or eat for dinner? Account for any differences in the appearance of the celery stalks. Explain your observations in terms of turgor pressure. Now do you understand why vegetables are sprayed in a supermarket?

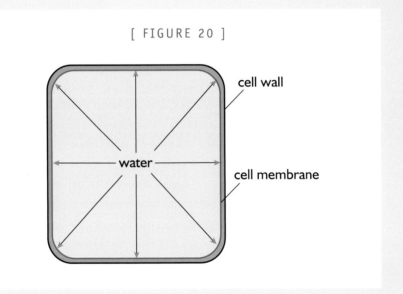

[FIGURE 20]

cell wall

water

cell membrane

As a plant cell fills with water, the water pushes against the cell membrane, which in turn pushes against the cell wall. This results in turgor pressure.

Science Fair Project Idea

Check with your science teacher for permission to use a microscope to carry out a project investigating turgor pressure in an aquatic plant. Change the environmental conditions to see what happens to turgor pressure in plant cells. Independent variables that you can change include the salt concentration of the water, lighting conditions, and carbon dioxide concentration. You can also investigate the role that turgor pressure plays in thigmonastic movements. These are movements that plants demonstrate in response to touching or shaking. Perhaps you are familiar with a well-known example, the folding of the leaves of a Venus flytrap in response to touch.

Materials:

- an adult
- 1 package of gelatin dessert
- pot
- stove
- water
- refrigerator
- fresh pineapple slice
- small dish

Life depends on chemical reactions. For example, the human body could not survive without the chemical reactions that control digestion, respiration, and excretion. In fact, the human body can be considered a chemical factory in which numerous chemical reactions take place. But these chemical reactions would not take place without the help of enzymes. An enzyme is an organic catalyst that speeds up the rate of a reaction. Enzymes are involved in the transport of carbon dioxide in the blood, the production of waste materials, and the digestion of foods.

Some enzymes are involved in the digestion of fats, a group of organic compounds that you read about in Chapters 1 and 2. Other enzymes help digest the two other kinds of organic compounds found in foods—carbohydrates (see Chapter 1) and proteins (see Chapter 2). Like fats, both carbohydrates and proteins contain the elements carbon, hydrogen, and oxygen. A protein also has the element nitrogen as part of its chemical makeup. In this experiment, you can explore how enzymes can digest a gelatin dessert, which is mostly protein.

Follow the instructions on the package to prepare a gelatin dessert. **You will need to boiling water, so ask an adult for help.** Once the gelatin has solidified take a small chunk and place it on a clean dish. Place a slice of fresh pineapple on top of the gelatin and observe what happens. Now you should realize why adding fresh pineapple to a gelatin dessert is not a good idea.

As proteins are digested by enzymes, more complex substances break into simpler substances. As these smaller molecules form, the solid gelatin turns into a liquid. Does pineapple have the same effect on carbohydrates? To find out, place a slice of pineapple on a cut potato, which is mostly carbohydrate. Also check to see whether the way fruit is prepared makes a difference. Observe what happens when you use frozen, cooked, canned, or dried pineapple in place of fresh pineapple. Try other fruits, such as an apple, grapefruit, cantaloupe, or pear, to see whether they have the same effect on proteins.

Do you think meat tenderizers work in a similar way?

5.4 How Does Meat Tenderizer Affect Protein?

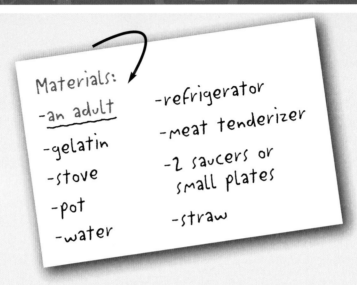

Materials:
- an adult
- gelatin
- stove
- pot
- water
- refrigerator
- meat tenderizer
- 2 saucers or small plates
- straw

Maybe you have eaten a tough piece of beef. Perhaps you are already aware that meat tenderizer can be sprinkled on tough meat to soften it. Did you ever wonder how meat tenderizer works? Try the following experiment to see what tenderizer does to protein, which is the main component of meat. Use gelatin rather than meat, because the effect is easier to observe. In fact, this experiment is very similar to the one in Experiment 5.3 where fresh fruit was placed on top of gelatin.

Prepare gelatin according to the directions on the package. **Ask an adult** to boil the water you need to dissolve the gelatin. Divide the solid gelatin into two pieces. Place each piece on a saucer. Sprinkle some meat tenderizer on one piece until there is a thin layer covering the gelatin. Allow the two pieces to remain undisturbed for 5 to 10 minutes. Then gently poke the gelatin pieces with a straw. Explain your observations.

Think back to Experiment 5.3. What was present in the fresh fruit that caused the gelatin to liquefy? What must be present in meat tenderizer? Why is it advisable to allow especially tough meat and tenderizer to stand for a few hours before broiling or barbecuing the meat? Test other household products such as vinegar and lemon juice for their ability to tenderize meats.

Materials:

-an adult

-60 g (2 oz)
 ground beef

-sensitive balance
 or scale

-baking sheet

-oven

-oven mitt

-microwave

-drinking glass

-cheesecloth

Beef tastes good because of the fats it contains. However, too much fat is not only unhealthy but also responsible for giving foods a greasy taste. The amount of fat permitted in certain foods is regulated by law. For example, the maximum for ground beef is 30 percent. For lean beef, it is 15 percent. How does the beef in your supermarket compare to those figures? The following experiment will give you the answer, but be warned: this experiment could stink up your kitchen.

Weigh 60 g (about 2 oz) of uncooked ground beef. Spread the beef out on a baking sheet and, **under adult supervision**, place it in the oven for 30 minutes at 105°C (220°F). The heat will evaporate the water in the meat. Allow the meat to cool. Remove the meat from the tray and weigh it. Subtract the weight of the dehydrated meat from the weight of the uncooked meat. The difference represents the weight of the water in the original meat sample.

Place the dehydrated meat in a piece of cheesecloth. Suspend the cheesecloth over a glass, as shown in Figure 21. Place the glass and the meat in a microwave. Microwave the meat until it looks dry and shriveled. The microwave will extract the fat from the meat. Some of the fat will collect as a liquid in the glass. The rest will vaporize. (**Ask an adult** if you should do this step outside on a porch or patio so that the vapors do not make the kitchen smell bad.)

Allow the meat to cool, remove it from the cheesecloth, and weigh it. Subtract the weight of the microwaved meat from the weight of the

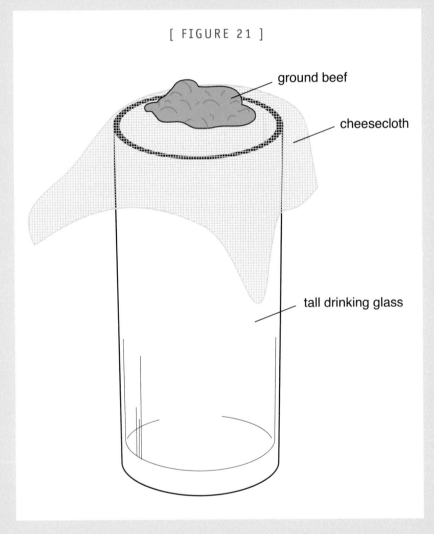

[FIGURE 21]

ground beef

cheesecloth

tall drinking glass

As the meat is microwaved, fats will liquefy and pass through
the cheesecloth into the glass. The high heat may vaporize
some of the fat, producing a foul smell.

dehydrated meat. This represents the mass of the fat in the original meat sample. Determine the percent of fat in your meat sample by using the following formula:

$$\frac{\text{weight of fat}}{\text{weight of dehydrated meat}} \times 100 = \text{percent fat}$$

Once you know how much water and fat are in meat, you may wonder where the beef is. Keep in mind that this procedure will give you only a rough idea of the fat content of meat. Using a microwave is not the best way to extract the fats from meat.

 ## Science Fair Project Idea

Extracting the fat from meat is possible if you do what chemists do—use a solvent. Because fats and water do not mix, you must use a solvent that dissolves grease. Such a solvent must be nonpolar and organic, like fats. Recall the expression from Experiment 4.2 that "like dissolves like." Hexane is a good solvent to use to determine the fat content of a wide variety of beef products, including fast-food hamburgers and hot dogs. When mixed with meat, hexane will dissolve the fats that are present. The hexane can then be evaporated, leaving the fats.

Be sure to carry out this project under a teacher's supervision. Weigh out 25 g of meat. Chop the meat into the smallest pieces possible and cover them with hexane. **Do not use hexane near a heat source because it is flammable.** Because hexane also evaporates fairly quickly and produces an odor, use a fume hood.

Stir the meat and hexane as thoroughly as possible for 15 to 20 minutes. Then filter everything through cheesecloth to

(continued on next page)

(continued from previous page)

collect the hexane. The hexane will have a yellowish color because of the fats that it contains. Collect the hexane in a clean container that you have weighed. Use a large, broad container, such as the one shown in Figure 22, because it will provide a large surface area to speed up the evaporation process. The hexane will slowly evaporate, leaving the fats in the container as a solid mass. Placing the container in the fume hood at school will speed up the process. Weigh the container after all the hexane has evaporated and calculate how much fat you extracted. Divide this value by the mass of the meat to get the percent fat.

While you have your meat samples, you may also want to check out their water content. How might you design an experiment to do this? Think about how you can make the water evaporate.

[FIGURE 22]

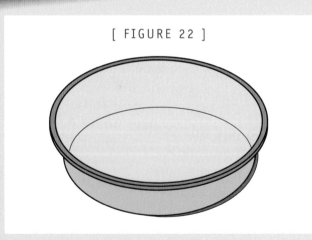

Scientists use an evaporating dish when they want to allow a liquid to evaporate. The wide surface allows the liquid to evaporate more quickly. Any solid materials are left behind in the dish.

CARBON DIOXIDE AND FIZZY SOLUTIONS

Flavored carbonated beverages are called soda or soda pop because an early method of making the CO_2 involved reacting carbonate of soda (Na_2CO_3, also called sodium carbonate) or bicarbonate of soda ($NaHCO_3$, also called sodium bicarbonate, or baking soda) with acid. Carbonated water is sometimes called seltzer water.

Carbon dioxide gas makes up about 0.04 percent of Earth's atmosphere. This gas has no odor and no color and will not burn. If the pressure is increased to 50 times the normal pressure of our atmosphere, then gaseous CO_2 will change to liquid. Liquid CO_2 can be stored in steel tanks. Bottling companies use it in liquid form.

Solubility is a measure of the ability of a substance to dissolve or go into a liquid. More CO_2 gas will dissolve in water as the water becomes colder. Carbon dioxide also dissolves more readily (becomes more soluble) as the pressure of the carbon dioxide gas above the water increases. In 1803, William Henry showed that the solubility of gas becomes greater as the pressure of the gas is increased. This general principle later came to be called Henry's law. Because of these temperature and pressure effects, carbonated water is made and bottled using high-pressure carbon dioxide and cold water. The pressure at which some carbonated beverages are sealed is about three times the normal pressure of the atmosphere. The volume of CO_2 gas when released from the carbonated liquid may be two to five times the volume of the liquid.

Naturally occurring carbonated mineral waters were known in ancient times and considered to be of medical benefit. Flemish chemist Jan Baptista van Helmont (1580–1644) discovered carbon dioxide. Joseph Priestley, a famous English chemist who later moved to America, found in 1767 that CO_2 dissolved in water gave it an "acidulated" taste that people enjoyed. William Brownrigg, an English physician, presented a paper before the Royal Society (a British scientific society) in 1765 about his experimentation with the "Mineral Elastic Spirit" (air) contained in spa water.

In America, the first carbonated waters were manufactured in 1807. Many countries around the world developed a carbonated water industry. By 1835, there were 64 carbonated water bottling facilities in the United States. By 1875 this number had increased to 512. By 1957 there were 5,200 bottling facilities for carbonated beverages, just in the United States.

As flavors were added to carbonated water, the drinks became more popular and the soft drink industry grew rapidly. The industry also developed because of technological advancements. Improvements in the production of liquid CO_2 allowed bottlers to buy it in tanks instead of making it themselves. The crown cap invented by William Painter in 1892 provided a reliable method of sealing glass bottles. Machine-made bottles allowed all bottles to be exactly the same, so machines could be developed for cleaning, filling, and capping the identical bottles.

Commercial bottlers normally get syrup flavors from another company. They use liquid CO_2 stored in metal tanks. They add this CO_2 to chilled water to make carbonated water. They place the syrup in a can or bottle, add the carbonated water, and seal the container. When you get a carbonated drink at a fast-food restaurant and fill your cup, you are doing something like what the bottlers do. When you press a button, CO_2 is mixed with water and syrup on its way to your cup.

In the next two experiments, you will explore some fascinating properties of CO_2 gas and the foam that it creates. The next time you open a soda, you may think differently about what's inside!

Materials:

- plastic 0.5-liter (500-ml) bottle of cola
- one-gallon resealable bag
- sink
- permanent marker
- measuring container marked in milliliters
- water

In this simple experiment, you will capture all the carbon dioxide gas that escapes from a carbonated beverage after it is opened. The object of this experiment is to measure the amount of gas released from a carbonated soda and compare it to the amount of starting liquid.

Place an unopened 500-ml bottle of cola inside a large resealable bag. Press down to seal the plastic bag, but leave a small opening in the corner. Now, push down on the bag to remove as much air as possible from inside the bag. You want the bag to be flat except where it surrounds the bottle. After you have flattened the bag, seal the bag completely.

Hold the bottle through the bag and carefully twist the cap. Holding the cap through the bag, twist a little at a time until you completely remove the cap. Tilt the bottle and bag to pour all the liquid out of the bottle and into the sealed bag.

Observe the bag for a few minutes. What do you see? Holding the bag over a sink, shake the bag a few times and then set it down.

Let the bag sit undisturbed in the sink for 1 hour and then check it again. Does the bag contain more liquid or more gas? There are 500 milliliters of liquid in the bag. Can you guess how much gas is in the bag?

Here is a method that you can use to measure the amount of gas trapped in the bag. Roll one side of the gas-filled bag as far as it will go until it is tight. Mark a line on the bag with a permanent marker at the place where the bag is rolled (see Figure 23). Open the bag, and remove

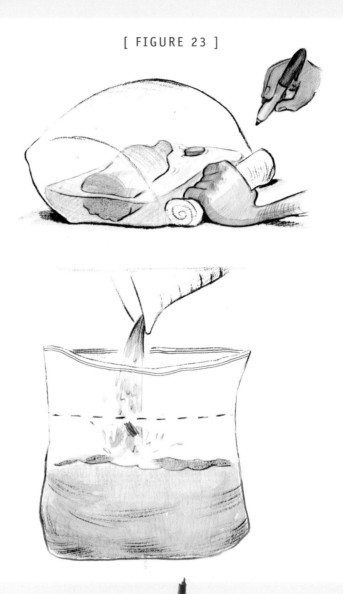

[FIGURE 23]

Roll one side of the gas-filled bag until it is tight. Mark a line on the sealed bag with a permanent marker at the place where the bag is rolled. Use this mark to determine how much carbon dioxide is trapped in the bag.

the empty bottle and cap but leave the liquid cola in the bag. Keeping careful track of the total amount of water, add water from a measuring container until the bag is filled up to your mark. The volume of water that you added to reach the mark is the same as the volume of gas that was trapped inside the bag.

Although the bag contained only one-half a liter of liquid, you may find that the bag contained two or more liters of gas. How could so much gas come from so little liquid?

In a closed soda bottle, water molecules surround molecules of carbon dioxide. Some carbon dioxide also combines with water to make carbonic acid. When you open a soft drink bottle, carbon dioxide gas that is dissolved in the water bubbles out of the liquid. Molecules in a liquid are close together, but molecules in a gas are far apart. As the carbon dioxide gas leaves the liquid, it fills the empty bag. A small volume of carbon dioxide dissolved in the liquid can fill a much larger volume as free gas. Most of the volume occupied by a gas is actually empty space between the moving molecules.

Science Fair Project Ideas

- Repeat this experiment with as many different brands of carbonated sodas as you can locate. Make a table with four columns labeled Drink name, Volume of liquid, Volume of gas, and Ratio of gas volume to liquid. Measure the volumes as you did in Experiment 5.6 and fill in the information in the table. To find the ratio of gas volume to liquid, divide the volume of gas by the volume of liquid. This division gives you the ratio of milliliters of gas per milliliter of liquid. This ratio allows you to compare drinks that may come in different sized bottles.

- You may be able to repeat the above experiment using different carbonated drinks that come in cans. However, you will have to be careful not to tear the bag as you open the can. Try as many different drinks as you can to compare the amount of carbonation. You can compare amounts of gas found in plastic bottles and aluminum cans for the same drink.

Materials:

- unopened bottle of cola
- liquid measuring cup
- tall, clear drinking glass
- stopwatch or watch or clock with a second hand
- sink
- milk (Keep refrigerated until ready to use.)

Have you ever poured soda into a glass and watched foam form and then disappear? Did you know that ice cream is a type of frozen foam? Ice cream contains ice crystals; liquid water with dissolved sugars, salts, and proteins; and foam made of trapped air bubbles. The frozen foam of trapped air bubbles makes the ice cream soft and fluffy. The object of this activity is to measure the lifetime of foam under different conditions and to determine how you can lengthen this lifetime.

Open a bottle of cola and gently pour 1/2 cup into a liquid measuring cup. Next, rapidly pour this cola into an empty drinking glass. You should see foam forming as soon as you pour the cola into the glass. Trapped bubbles of carbon dioxide gas escape from the soda when it is poured, creating the foam. The foam may not last long because the bubbles break and the carbon dioxide gas escapes into the air. Use a stopwatch to measure exactly how long the foam remains on top of the liquid before it disappears. Start measuring the time as soon as you dump the soda into the glass.

Pour all the liquid out of the glass into the sink and rinse the glass with water. Dry the glass. Now add 1/2 cup of cold milk to the empty glass. Rinse the measuring cup with water. As you did previously, gently pour 1/2 cup of cola into the measuring cup. Next, rapidly pour this cola into the drinking glass holding the milk. Time how long the foam remains on the top of the liquid before it disappears.

Repeat the above step using 1/4 cup of milk and 1/2 cup of cola. Repeat again using 1/8 cup of milk and 1/2 cup of cola. Rinse and dry the glass and measuring cup after each experiment. For every new milk and cola combination, time how long the foam lasts. When you do the 1/8 cup milk and 1/2 cup cola combination, look carefully at the foam through the side of the glass. Does the collection of larger bubbles, with each bubble surrounded by others, look something like a honeycomb? Watch it for several minutes. Describe what you see and how it changes with time.

In your science notebook, make a table with columns labeled Amount of milk, Amount of cola, and Lifetime of the foam (see Table 1). Repeat all the cola and milk combinations several times. Find the average foam life-times for each different combination and record it in the fourth column.

Milk is a complex mixture that contains mostly water along with sugar, proteins, and fat. There are also salts and vitamins present in milk. The amount of fat in milk can vary, but it is listed on the milk carton as 1 percent, 2 percent, 4 percent, and so forth.

When a carbonated soda is poured into milk, the protein molecules and fat globules in the milk surround the carbon dioxide gas bubbles. The proteins and fat form a thin film that makes the walls of the foam. The film holds the carbon dioxide gas trapped and provides the structure of the foam. As time passes, the smaller bubbles break and form larger bubbles. Larger bubbles have less pressure inside and are more stable than small ones. Gradually, the larger bubbles also break and the foam disappears.

Bubbles don't last long with just pure cola because it lacks the supporting protein and fat molecules. As you add some milk, the foam

TABLE 1.

Average Lifetime of Foam

Amount of Milk	Amount of Cola	Lifetime of Foam	Average Lifetime of Foam
0	½ cup	trial 1:	
		trial 2:	
		trial 3:	
½ cup	½ cup	trial 1:	
		trial 2:	
		trial 3:	
¼ cup	½ cup	trial 1:	
		trial 2:	
		trial 3:	
⅛ cup	½ cup	trial 1:	
		trial 2:	
		trial 3:	

should last longer. However, if you add too much milk, the foam lifetime gets shorter. Why? Colder milk also helps to support the fat-filled foam.

Proteins from barley help maintain the head (foamy top) on poured beer. The proteins create a network around the bubbles and help them last longer. Beer contains carbon dioxide gas that makes it fizz. Some beers have nitrogen gas added to help make more foam.

Have you seen the foam on ocean waves as they break on shore? Proteins coming from seaweed in the ocean help to provide the walls of this air-filled foam.

 Science Fair Project Ideas

- Repeat this experiment with different amounts of cola and milk until you find the combination that gives the longest-lasting foam. Explore the difference between using cold milk and warm milk.
- Repeat the experiment using different samples of milk containing various percentages of fat, such as 1 percent, 2 percent, and 4 percent. Does changing the amount of fat change the foam lifetime? Does changing the amount of fat in the milk affect the amount of milk that gives the longest-lasting foam?

FURTHER READING

Books

Bochinski, Julianne Blair. *The Complete Workbook for Science Fair Projects.* Hoboken, N.J.: John Wiley and Sons, Inc., 2005.

Levine, Shar, and Leslie Johnstone. *Kitchen Science.* New York: Sterling Publishing Co., 2003.

Moorman, Thomas. *How to Make Your Science Project Scientific.* Revised Edition. New York: John Wiley & Sons, Inc., 2002.

O'Leary, Nancy K., and Susan Shelly. *The Complete Idiot's Guide to Science Fair Projects.* New York: Alpha Books, 2003.

Shanley, Ellen, and Colleen Thompson. *Fueling the Teen Machine.* Palo Alto, Calif.: Bull Publishing Co., 2001.

Townsend, John. *Crazy Chemistry.* Mankato, Minn.: Raintree, 2007.

Internet Addresses

Institute of Food Technologists. *Introduction to the Food Industry.* **2008.**
http://www.ift.org/cms/?pid=1000411

Society for Science and the Public. *Science News for Kids.* **2008.**
http://www.sciencenewsforkids.org

United States Department of Agriculture. *MyPyramid.gov.* **2008.**
http://www.mypyramid.gov

INDEX

A

acids, 73–74, 77
adipose tissue, 42
albumin, 45
Alzheimer's disease, 54
amino acids, 45–46
anencephaly, 55–56
ascorbic acid (vitamin C), 55, 57–59, 103

B

baking powder, 61, 74
baking soda, 61, 73–79
Baptista van Helmont, Jan, 115
Benedict's solution, 28
beriberi, 52–53
birth defects, 55–56
Biuret test, 48
Brownrigg, William, 115
butter, 87–90, 93–95

C

calciferol (vitamin D), 53, 55–56
calcium, 51, 97
Calories/calories, 32–35, 38
calorimeters, 33–35
carbohydrates
    heat effects, 30–35
    overview, 20–22, 108
    sources of, 23–25
    testing for, 27–29
carbonated beverages, 102, 115–119
carbon dioxide production, 62–66, 73–74, 77
catalysts, 69–72, 108
cellulose, 22
cheese making, 83–85
chemical formula, 89
chlorine, 52
chlorophyll, 24, 25
clay, 79
Clinistix, 28
cobalt chloride, 32

colloids, 81–85
combustion, 69–72
copper, 52
copper sulfate solution, 48

D

decomposition, 69–72
disaccharides, 22

E

Eijkman, Christiaan, 52
emulsifiers, 99–100
emulsion, 99–100
endothermic reactions, 69–72
energy
    brain requirements, 14
    fermentation, 63
    from food, 16–17, 20–22, 32–39
    measurement of, 32–39
enzymes, 41, 53, 108–109
exothermic reactions, 69–72
experiments, designing, 8–9

F

fats
    chemistry of, 87–89
    energy in, 35
    oils, 87–89, 91–95
    overview, 20, 41, 42, 108
    saturated, 87, 91
    testing for, 43–44, 111–113
    unsaturated, 87, 91–95
fatty acids, 87–90
fermentation, 63
fire, 13
fire extinguishers, 77–78
fluorine, 52
folic acid (folacin), 54–55
food
    drying, 15–16
    energy from, 16–17, 20–22, 32–39
    overview, 13–14
    preservation, 103–106

snacks, 35
sources of, 17, 18
types of, 20–22
fruits, preservation of, 103–104
fungi, 63
Funk, Casimir, 52

G

gelatin, 108–109
glucose, 63, 67–68
glue, 86

H

hemoglobin, 45
Henry's law, 115
Henry, William, 115
hexane, 93, 113–114
Hopkins, Frederick, 53
hunter-gatherer society, 13–14
hydrogenated vegetable oil, 87
hydrogenation, 93–95
hydrogen peroxide, 69–72
hypothesis, 8

I

indophenol, 58
iodine, 25, 28, 51–52, 91
iron, 51, 97

L

lactic acid, 83, 85
lactose, 22, 83, 85
leavening agents, 61
leaves, 23–24
lipids, 87–90

M

magnesium, 52, 97
margarine, 87–90, 93–95
methylphytylnaphthoquinone
    (vitamin K), 56
minerals, 41–42, 51–52, 97–98
molecules, polarity in, 93

monosaccharides, 20–22, 28

N

niacin (vitamin B_3), 54

O

observations, qualitative vs.
    quantitative, 89–90
oils, 87–89, 91–95

P

Painter, William, 116
Pauling, Linus, 55
pellagra, 54
phosphorus, 51, 97
photometers, 44
photosynthesis, 23–25
pigment, 23–25, 55, 101
polysaccharides, 22
potassium, 52
proteins
    digestion of, 108, 110
    energy in, 35
    overview, 20, 41, 45–46
    testing for, 47–48
    Tyndall effect, 49–50
Priestly, Joseph, 115
pyridoxine (vitamin B_6), 54

R

rennin, 85
retinol (vitamin A), 53, 55
riboflavin (vitamin B_2), 53–54
rickets, 52, 56

S

safety, 11, 25, 28, 58
science fairs, 10
scientific method, 8–9
scurvy, 52, 55
snack foods, 35
Snowdon, David, 54
sodium, 52

sodium hydroxide solution, 48
solubility, 115
solutions, 81
solvents, 93, 113–114
spina bidifa, 55–56
starch, 22, 24–25, 28, 67–68
structural formula, 89
sucrose, 22, 63, 67–68
sugars, 20–22, 28–29, 63–68

T

temperature effects, 30–35, 69–72,
    81–82
theory, 8
thyroxin, 51
tocopherol (vitamin E), 53, 56
tools, 14
Turgor pressure, 105
Tyndall effect, 49–50
Tyndall, John, 49

V

variables, 9
vegetable oils, 87–89, 91–95

vegetables, preservation of, 105–106
vegetarians, 17
vitamin K, 53, 56
vitamins, 52–59. *See also* specific
    vitamins.

W

water, 20, 45

Y

yeast
    carbon dioxide production by, 62–66
    as catalyst, 69–72
    overview, 61, 63
    sugar metabolism by, 63, 67–68

Z

zinc, 52, 97